# *Farewell Mr John*

**'A Lifetime of Memories'**

Author

Ronald E. Hepting

## Dedications

I dedicate this book to my family and hope that it may bring pleasure to all who read it.

First and foremost, I would like to thank you all for your support, caring and absolute devotion to my cause. You were there when I needed you most and I cannot thank you enough. My son Kevin, my wonderful daughter Dawn, my son in law Kim, my daughter in law Sally and Sally's mum Bernie. I really don't know what I'd have done without you. Thank you from the bottom of my heart.

I hope you enjoy reading about my journey and will tell my grandchildren and great grandchildren about my life. I've made lots of friends along the way and I thank you all for your support, Carole, Kim Edwards and members of my own family who sadly I've only got to know through bereavements. We have such a wonderful, large family and my last words must be to you all, please be proud to be a member of the Hepting family as I'm totally sure you are.

# CONTENTS

# The Hepting Family Tree

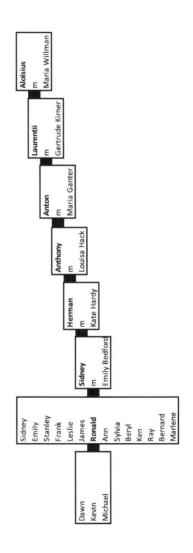

# 1

## My arrival in the family

Ronald Edward Hepting, I arrived in this world on 10th September 1936 at 52 Tewkesbury Road, Tottenham, London, born to parents, Emily (nee Bedford) and Sidney Hepting. That was eighty-three years ago, at the time of finishing my story, I don't remember too much about it though!

My memoirs start from the age of three in 1939 at the outbreak of World War II. I was born one of fourteen children, nine boys and five girls. I came seventh as there were six older siblings, Sidney, Emily (known as Sissy to all), Stanley (known as Bill), Frank, Leslie and James and six younger than me, Ann (known to all as Barbara), Sylvia (known as Sylvie), Beryl, Kenneth (known as Ginger, due to his red hair), Raymond (known as Cod, a name given to him when he was young because his eyes were large and dark) and Bernard (known as Monty).

The fourteenth child, Marlene, unfortunately only survived for three months, she was born with Down's syndrome. How my parents, especially my mother, coped with that loss I shall never know.

I attended Vale Road Nursery School in Tottenham, just around the corner to our house. This was the first nursery school to open in Tottenham, in 1937. In later years, my mother told me how I would sit on my teachers lap and sing to her, even at that tender age.

**The War Years 1939-1945**

At the outbreak of war in 1939 parents were torn whether or not to evacuate their children to different locations around the country, mostly to rural areas, so that they would be safe from the horrendous bombing campaign that was expected to take place across London, the surrounding boroughs and all big cities and towns in Great Britain. There were conflicting views especially from some mothers and parents who opted to keep their children at home. Some even wondered how anyone could send their children to live with complete strangers. The view of any parent and a mother's instinct is always to protect her children and because of the fear bombs raining down on London and other major cities, the majority were evacuated to relative safety. My own family had the three elder brothers in the forces at one time or another during the course of the war. My elder sister Sissy stayed at home, the rest of us were evacuated at the beginning of the war, eight children in all. At the end of the war every member of the family had survived.

My dad was an Air Raid warden during the war years which must have been terrifying, to be out in the pitch dark streets when bombs and incendiaries (fire bombs) were falling all around.

# 2

## Separated from my family

Because of the war and before I had the chance to get to know my family some of us were evacuated, along with thousands of other children to different parts of the country. My brothers, Jim, Bill and Leslie, who were two, four and nine years older than me, went to Cornwall on the north coast and my sister, Sylvie and I went to Rutland.

We were taken there by train and then on to the local Manor House in a small village called Braunston where we waited for someone to come and pick us up. This is where Sylvie and I were separated. I didn't know where my sister went, I wasn't told.

I was chosen by John and Mary Addison. A couple in their forties, who lived and farmed at Chestnut Farm nearby. They became my 'adopted' parents for most of my stay in Braunston.

As I was so young and because I didn't really know my own parents it didn't take me too long to accept them and their way of life. A lot of what happened during the next five to six years stayed with me for the rest of my life. John and Mary were a very kind couple, although would at the same time chastise and correct me if I was in the wrong or misbehaved. I was never mistreated in any way and soon got to know the local children of my age. I started to bond and become great pals with them, all except one, an American kid. He would brag about his dad being a pilot in the American Air Force. I took an instant dislike to him as he had an arrogant attitude. His name was Mark Freeman and he said his dad was over here to fight for the English. For some reason I saw red at this remark and laid into him with both hands. We were in the school playground at the time and finished up rolling about in a clump of stinging nettles. When the school head found out she told me to say sorry to him. I refused.

It was quite an adventure for me and for most kids that were evacuated during this time as we had never seen the countryside, cows, pigs or even chickens and geese. As I got more used to it I came to love the way of life in the country. We were very close to an American air base and the sound of the bomber aircraft flying overhead was really noisy and pretty scary. By now I was quite pally with several of the local lads and although there wasn't a lot to do after school we would go fishing or climb trees. On the odd occasion we would see a plane come down in a plume of smoke and if it wasn't too far away we would run across the fields to the crash site.

I must say I saw some grisly sights but all we were interested in was the Perspex windows of the cockpit which we would make rings out of. There was one particular spot I would go to and watch paratroopers jump out of a balloon in practice for the real thing.

I didn't know then that my brother Sidney, was a paratrooper, he joined up at seventeen, although the official age was eighteen. Many young men lied about their age to get into the army as it seemed glamorous compared to being a factory worker or painter. I was six years old now and the war had been going on for three years.

I'd got used to life in the village and would look forward to Monday evenings when we would load our lorry up with eggs and take them to Stamford for sale, this was the highlight of my week. Another event was the yearly harvest, this was such a very important occasion in the calendar and I couldn't wait for it to come round. A harvesting machine was used in the fields to cut the corn in ever decreasing circles. A shot would then be fired from a rifle and suddenly there were rabbits running everywhere. Needless to say the six crack shots with rifles had a field day and we had a good stock of rabbits and some delicious rabbit pies and rabbit stew.

There was always something to do on the farm and one of the many jobs was the daily collection of eggs from the nests of the chickens, ducks and geese. One particular morning I went into the barn to collect the geese eggs, my eye caught sight of what looked like a rat's tail hanging down over a wooden beam, being a six year old and having no fear, I grabbed hold of it and wouldn't let go, to my astonishment the rat shed its tail and I was left holding it. It belonged to the biggest rat I had ever seen.

I was now in my seventh year and was told by John and Mary that I was going to live with someone else. I was heartbroken and remember that I couldn't stop crying. I would be going to live with an elderly sister of the couple I had been living with. I was told it was just across the road from the farm and I could visit them whenever I wanted. This eased my pain somewhat, although there was nothing I could do about it.

However, I was not to be disappointed, she was a lovely lady and a very God fearing person. Her name was Elizabeth and she affectionately became known to me as Aunt Liz. I remember becoming very frightened of formations of bomber aircraft flying overhead at night and she would let me get into bed with her until they had passed. One day I was exercising in the school playground when I felt a sharp pain in my groin, it didn't take me too long to find out that I should not put my lunch in my trousers pocket, especially jam sandwiches.

After I deduced that I'd been stung by a jam loving wasp I was taken home for remedial treatment. There is obviously something to be said for old wives tales as after Aunt Liz fried some onions, let them cool and applied them to the said wound, the pain disappeared in no time and I had the rest of the day off school, yippee!

One thing I must mention is that just a few miles from my

home in Braunston was the town of Melton Mowbray, you've got it, the home of the most famous pork pies in the world. I was weaned on them and to this day haven't lost my taste for them.

I was now nearly nine years old and little did I know then that the war was coming to an end and so was the life I had come to love. I would now be torn away from my 'family' and the countryside which I'd come to think of as my home. How could this be when I felt that I was leaving, what were to me by now, my real parents, to go back to a place I didn't know. I was told that my real mum and dad would be waiting for me when I got back to London. I suppose it was the same for most of the evacuees, some of whom were probably a lot worse off than me.

On the morning of my departure, after my tearful goodbyes to Aunt Liz and John and Mary Addison who had become my family, and all my mates, I was taken to Oakham Station which is a couple of miles away from the village. I had a label on my coat with my name on and was carrying my gas mask, some sandwiches to eat on the way and a basket containing three little kittens named Torty, Blacky and Sandy. When the train pulled into the station I got on and took a seat next to the window and was quite oblivious to anything that was going on around me. I watched the fields, the cows, the sheep and the telegraph poles flying past me and heard the train whistle blowing. I suddenly felt the tears rolling down my face and was trying to look through the window that was steaming up from my breath. By this time everything had become a blur and I must have fallen asleep.

# 3

## Return to London

A voice, that seemed so far away suddenly seemed so loud, woke me saying "Ronald, time to wake up." It was a lady from the WRVS (Women's Royal Voluntary Service), they were responsible for escorting children back to their home cities. "Are you ok?" she asked. "Yes, I'm fine," I replied. The whole journey had seemed like a dream.

As the train slowed down, my view was now of grimy, damaged buildings and a smoky atmosphere which seemed very depressing after the clean air, colour and openness of the countryside.

My heart was now pumping faster with apprehension. The screeching wheels of the train now came to a halt and we were escorted to the station waiting room. I was joined there by another young girl who I was informed was my younger sister Sylvie. I didn't recognise her as I last saw her when I was three years old and six years had passed. We sat and waited and eventually a lady came, she took my hand and said, 'Come along Ronald'. It was my mother. The next thing I remember was boarding a trolley bus.

After what seemed like an age we got off the bus, walked down a hill to a small house at the bottom, this was my home and the place where I was born. I remember saying to my mother I want to go home and I cried bitterly, telling her that I wanted to go back to Aunt Liz.

There was an acrid smell in the air, I was told it was gas, it made me feel sick.

## Bonding with my family

I hadn't had any contact with my brothers or sisters for the duration of the war and so they were like strangers to me. I began bonding with them as soon as I felt comfortable. My two elder brothers Jim and Les being two and four years older than me were very streetwise and I wanted to be like them. I would follow them wherever they went but it was quite obvious they didn't want me around. On one occasion Jim spotted me and called me over, he told me that if I wanted to go with them, I would have to go home, tidy myself up and they would wait for me to come back. Needless to say, when I got back they were gone! I fell for this several times but eventually they decided to wait for me.

One Sunday morning we walked to Stamford Hill, to the cinema called the Regent which was about a mile walk from our house. The three of us went up an alleyway to a side door, Leslie went around to the front door to wait for the people to come out, which signalled the end of the programme. He would then ask someone to take him into the cinema, being a minor, he'd then go straight to the toilet and push the bar up on the side door to let us in, this was known as bunking in.

I had never been to the pictures before, so this was a new experience for me. The film was called *Blue Skies*, a musical, starring Bing Crosby and Joan Caulfield. After that day, learning how to bunk in, I became one of the gang.

It was coming up to my tenth birthday and the family had been offered a three bedroom council house at Tottenham Hale.

I'm sure Tottenham stood still on the day we moved. I remember we hired about eight coster monger barrows at sixpence a time to move home. Our procession down Seven Sisters Road into Broad Lane brought N15 and N17 to a halt.

It was now 1946 and there had been an addition to our family the previous year, my brother Monty, making a total of thirteen children in all, nine boys and four girls.

During my time in the country I had picked up the local tongue and spoke with a Leicestershire lingo. I was ribbed about this by my two elder brothers but the accent tended to disappear after a couple of years.

My new school was called Down Lane which was in Park View Road at the bottom of Chestnut Road and was a ten minute walk from where I lived. I spent a year there before moving to Page Green School in Broad Lane. My two elder brothers also attended the same school, so I was in good hands. The next two or three years were quite uneventful but fruitful in making new friends.

At fourteen years old I was becoming fashion and girl conscious. I guess at that age you are still pretty vulnerable and prone to fall in love pretty easily. I met a young lady in the Tottenham Royal, a dance hall, and she became my dance partner. Her name was Maureen and we got on very well. This was the 1950's and soon to be the age of Rock 'n' Roll.

The early 1950's was the era of the big bands and those of my age would remember Ted Heath, Joe Loss, Jack Parnell and the Ray Ellington Quartet. Every Thursday at the Royal was talent night and I was always one of the first to put my name down to enter the competition. The big stars of that era were Frankie Laine, Johnnie Ray, Billy Daniels, Dickie Valentine, Dennis Lotis and Lita Rosa to name but a few.

I was a singer impersonator and would imitate the stars of the day. During this time I got to know another singer who did the same, although I have to say that he was better, his name was Ray Livermore. I first met Ray in a social club called Copes in Commercial Road, Edmonton. I was the first contestant in a talent competition, my song was *Sunny Side of the Street*, made famous by Frankie Laine. I won the competition and my prize was fifteen pounds worth of savings stamps and a bottle of Stingo which was a very strong ale. This was my first success as a singer and from then on that was to be my vocation in life. I was now finding that music was my first love and I wanted to be a singer.

My younger brother Ken and I decided to go out and buy a guitar, learn a few chords and form our own skiffle group. We went to a second hand music shop in West Green Road called the Swap Shop. We both had a fiver in our pocket and came away with one Spanish and one acoustic guitar. We bought a book called Play the Guitar by Bert Weedon.

Ginger and I practiced the chords until we'd learnt enough to be able to form our own group. For those who don't know what skiffle music is, it's American folk music improvised with a couple of guitars, a washboard played with thimbles, a string bass made with a tea chest and the lyrics.

With Ginger and I on guitar, our eldest brother Sid on washboard and our dad on bass we started busking outside Wards Corner and Seven Sisters Road as the cinemas and the Royal Dance Hall turned out. We had a cardboard box where onlookers would throw coins and sometimes the odd bit of paper money. It was great fun until the police moved us on. As we got better and more ambitious, we decided to reach for the stars and took on an agent.

Meanwhile I got myself a Saturday job working for my uncle. He lived in Church Road, opposite Park Lane, Tottenham, next to the Spurs ground. Every other Saturday when Spurs were at home, he would use his back garden to store cycles. Cycling was a popular means of transport then and for every bike he took in he charged sixpence. It was my job to stand outside and accost the cyclists. A raffle ticket would be given to them and the other half of the ticket stuck on their bike. I got two shillings and sixpence to do this but after a while I wanted to go to the game myself so stopped doing it.

# 4

## The Finsbury Park Empire

It seemed we were all quite talented musically so we decided to write to Hughie Green, a TV presenter and talent scout. We were amazed a couple of weeks later to get a reply and were given a specific date to go for an audition at the Civic Theatre at Poplar. We were excited at the prospect and made our own way by bus to the venue.

Watching some of the other acts we thought we had a reasonable chance. The judging was done by a machine called a clapometer which meant the louder the audience clapped the better your chances. We knew we were in with a chance until a ten year old girl took the plaudits with her tap dancing. We came second and were told to polish up our act and try again at a later date. We didn't go back but instead entered a South East Counties Skiffle competition.

The preliminary heats were to be held in Granada Cinemas all over London. After having got through every round to the semi-final we would have to appear at the Granada Cinema, Edmonton. Between appearing at Poplar and entering this competition we had dispensed with our female vocalist and acquired the services of another.

We went on to win the semi-final and now had a place in the final. We were duly notified of the date and venue of the final which was to be held at none other than the Finsbury Park Empire. The Finsbury Park Empire stood on the corner of St. Thomas Road and Prah Road and was considered the London Palladium of North London.

Opening in 1910, all the stars of the era played the venue including in the early days, Laurel and Hardy, George Formby, Marie Lloyd and later, Dean Martin, Jerry Lewis, Shirley Bassey and in its closing years Dusty Springfield. The Cliff Richard film *The Young Ones* included scenes shot inside and outside of the Empire. Sadly in 1965 the building was demolished, and a council housing block now stands there. There is an Islington People's Plaque on the building commemorating the theatre which played a big part in the lives of those who went there and who voted to have the plaque placed there.

Come the day, we arrived at the theatre and were allowed to walk out on stage just to get the feeling of appearing on one of the biggest stages in the country. We were absolutely awe struck but so looking forward to our big night whatever happened. We were quietly confident and hoped that we would do well. We were introduced to the two judges who were Jim Dale, a singer and star of the Carry On films and childrens' TV entertainer, Wally Whyton. We were the one but last of the acts to perform and we took our place on stage before the curtains went up. We couldn't see a thing, the footlights dazzled and then the audience was clapping and cheering, I'm sure half of Tottenham was there to support us. There was a distinct hush in the crowd as we went into our song.

At that time Skiffle music was very popular and one particular group, Chas McDevitt and his female vocalist Nancy Whiskey, had already had a massive hit with a number called *Freight Train*. We decided to sing the B side of that record called *Face in the Rain*. After our performance we were pretty confident.

We waited some time before the two judges gave out the result. We were dumbfounded when the winning group was announced, we came second yet again and unfairly we thought. We objected to the result, our reasons were that the group that won was not a Skiffle group and had sung an Everly Brothers song called *Wake up little Susie* which we argued was a Rock 'n' Roll song. After some further deliberation by the judges, the result of the competition stood and we were very disappointed.

Our interest in music had now taken over and Ginger and I started entertaining in pubs and clubs.

Meanwhile life went on and I would go to my local youth club at Bruce Grove called, Lynch House. It was there that I first met Dave Clark who later became famous as the lead of Dave Clark Five. He was a local lad from Philip Lane in Tottenham.

Ginger and I became regulars at The Fountain pub in West Green Road, Tottenham. The compere there was a man known as Charlie Smithers, he later became one of the comedians on a TV programme of the same name called The Comedians. Every time my brother and I walked into the pub he introduced us as Ron and Ken and would call us onto the stage later in the evening.

Ginger felt that he wasn't a vocalist and wanted me to sing and he would play guitar. I convinced him one evening to do an Everly Brothers song with me as we had practiced the harmony at home. We sang *Let it be Me,* it brought the house down and after that he never doubted his ability to sing as well as play.

Saturday was looming and I was now a regular at Spurs home games and I would walk through the back doubles from Tottenham Hale to White Hart Lane to the Spurs home ground with my eldest brother Sid which took about thirty minutes. I don't know how much he paid to get in but I do remember it cost me nine old pennies (there were 240 pennies to the pound then) to go into the boys section called The Shelf. Spurs were playing Sunderland in a First Division match and there wasn't a space left in the ground. I was privileged to have watched the great Len Shackleton play and can only say that he deserves his legend status.

At one particular part of the game Shackleton took possession of the ball and proceeded to juggle with it, his amazing skills stopped the game in its tracks as all the players stood and watched his artistry. A full minute elapsed before he kicked the ball back into play and the game continued to a thundering ovation.

Sometime later, for those who remember, Spurs had a diminutive, very skilled, player called, Tommy Harmer. The game was brought to another standstill as he displayed all his skills to an adoring sixty thousand plus crowd. I was privileged to have been at White Hart Lane on that occasion and I have never seen anything like it since.

# 5

## My sporting career

etween the years of 1947 and 1951 my mother worked in Stoke Newington as a house cleaner. Being a very under privileged family, to make ends meet, she had to go out and earn a few extra shillings so that we could have shoes and clothes for school. In 1949 I was chosen along with another pupil my age to spend a summer term at a boarding school down in Hampshire. I jumped at the opportunity to go and the other pupil was a young girl named Sylvia Keyes. Like me, she came from a big family, who were very musically orientated like us.

This was another adventure for me and as I had spent much of my life away from home it was no hardship for me. After three months I came home, I told my mother I liked it so much and could I go back for a second term. After checking it out with the authorities I was granted a second term at the boarding school. Eventually I had to come home though, rather reluctantly I might add.

I was now nearing school leaving age and heavily into sport. I was having javelin throwing lessons and being tutored by my sports teacher. I was also playing cricket and football for a local team called Castledean United. We played our home games on the Tottenham Marshes and had to carry the goal posts and crossbar from the changing rooms and set them up on the pitch. If you were playing on pitches running parallel to the River Lea you could always bank on losing one ball in the river.

I remember one Sunday morning we were playing a cup match in Finsbury Park. I don't remember who the opposition was except that they wore red shirts, this motivated me to the extreme and I went on to score ten goals from ten corners. As a centre forward, I have always wondered if that was a record and if it still stands to this day.

There were two talented footballers in the team, one who I went to school with, Donny Armstrong, and another boy named Donny Saggers. I don't know what happened to young Armstrong but I'm sure he went on to bigger and better clubs. As for Donny Saggers, he went on to play for the top amateur club, Walthamstow Avenue. Unfortunately, his footballing career came to a sad and abrupt end when he broke his leg whilst playing in an Amateur Cup Final at Wembley.

One incident stood out for me a couple of years before I left school. Whatever school you went to there was always a bully and Page Green was no exception, whenever there was a fight in the playground everyone would gather round in a circle and let them fight it out. On this occasion my brother Jim took on the bully, whose name I remember to this day, Fred Bontoft, no-one had dared challenge him before. Jim was very fit and did boxing as a schoolboy amateur. It was a bruising bare fisted encounter which went on for ten minutes or so until finally it was all over. The best man won and that was my brother Jim.

Each year there was an annual sports day for all the Tottenham schools and every year the three protagonists to win this exciting encounter were Rowland Hill, Risley Avenue and Page Green, where I was a pupil. The venue was Haringey Stadium. I was taking part in the javelin competition for which I'd trained twice a week with my sports teacher Mr McKay. I'm afraid to say I won by default as my opponent slipped and fell while throwing. The javelin failed to stick in so I still had to beat his previous throw which led the contest. This I did by inches and so won, ironically, he came from Rowland Hill

School which normally won all the certificates but this time I was awarded the winner's certificate. I became a hero back at school and for my exploits was made a prefect, which I hated. I could no longer get into trouble or bunk off school which I was accustomed to doing. I had to think of a plan to lose this unwanted, meritorious award and a chance soon presented itself.

During a change-over of lessons I always checked the contents of the desk I was sitting at. On opening the desk, I came across four pennies and nicked them. The person, whose desk it was, reported to their teacher that the coins had gone missing.

There was an immediate inquiry and I was identified as the person who sat at that desk. The whole class was asked to empty their pockets out while the contents were checked. I was found to have four pennies in my pocket that I swore were mine. The person who the coins belonged to had kept the dates of all the pennies and I had no defence.

I was summoned to the Headmaster's office and asked to explain what defence I had, if any. I had no answers. My punishment would be four strokes of the cane across my fingers. One stroke for every penny and I am so glad it wasn't more. It was very painful and brought tears to my eyes. I lost my prefect status as a result and could now be the disruptive pupil that my mates admired.

# 6

## Toasted cheese and rats

We lived in a house at 31 Station Road which was right next to Tottenham Hale Railway Station. The tube station didn't exist at that time and Station Road is no longer recognisable as the road we lived in, only the station and the now derelict pub on the corner at the other end of the road still stand.

The house and street were absolutely bug infested and it was no big deal to wake up at night with bugs in your bed and mice and rats scampering about on the floor and in the ceiling. At that time there were five of us sharing two beds in one room, five sharing another room and my parents in their own room.

One day Jim came in with a rat trap and we decided to put the trap in a hole in the ceiling. Before we all went to bed my brother toasted a piece of cheese and set the trap. We didn't have to wait long before we heard them scuttling about and with bated breath, waited for the trap to be sprung. After a couple of hours we must have fallen asleep. It wasn't as easy as we thought it was going to be and it took a whole week before we caught anything. The result was a rat about nine inches long.

We soon lost interest in this and decided to try different tactics. We had a Diana slug gun which shot lead pellets or tiny coloured darts. Using the same procedure, at bedtime we would toast a piece of cheese and put it next to a hole in the kitchen skirting board, we would take turns to wait for a mouse to emerge and then fire. This was our entertainment until we decided to go to bed. That's the way we and no doubt others in the street lived. Yes, we were poor but strangely enough we were happy. My mother made sure we never went without a meal but if you were to upset her you paid the penalty. I remember one time I bragged to all my mates that our best cups were jam jars, this was true, we did drink from jam jars but somehow or other it got back to my mother that I was responsible for telling my friends about how we lived. I am not ashamed to say that I got the biggest hiding of my life and was very careful after that not to divulge any information about the family.

When the winters were really cold it was a struggle to keep warm. With the railway on our doorstep there was always plenty of coal in the sidings and Jim, Les and myself would clamber over a wall which separated the railway track from the alleyway that led to Down Lane Park. Two of us would fill a couple of sacks with coal and drop them over the wall where we would carry them back to the house just a couple of hundred yards away. We all knew it was wrong to steal but it was survival, nothing more.

When Christmas came around the Tom Arnold's Circus would come to Haringey Arena. They always wanted labour from the local community for prop men and casual work. Jim got a job as caretaker of none other than Buffalo Bill's horse. So, we earned a few pennies while the circus was in town. It was very exciting for us as on opening night we got to meet some J Arthur Rank film stars and celebrities who appeared for charity purposes.

I shook hands with Jack Hawkins, Kenneth More, John Gregson, Kay Kendall and up and coming starlet June Thorburn. Tragically she was killed, aged thirty-six, in an Iberia plane crash at Blackdown, Sussex in 1967.

# 7

# Teddy Boys and villains

It was 1949 and the war had been over for four years. Although most things were still on rations, clothing coupons were now taken off rationing. This meant that I could now have a suit for the first time in my life at the age of thirteen. Mum took me to Wood Green Co-Op and I bought my first ever suit on the never never. This meant that it could be paid for by weekly instalments.

As the Edwardian style was all the rage at the time, I indulged myself in a Black Barathea Suit. The jacket was known as a drape, it came down to the knees with half-moon pockets and a velvet collar together with drain-pipe trousers. I felt I was the bee's knees and would put it on to go dancing at the Tottenham Royal where all the other teenagers would congregate and show off their suits. Collectively, we were called Teddy Boys. Unfortunately, because of a small hooligan element amongst the Teds, as they became known, we were all tarred with the same brush and got a bad reputation.

Nothing very eventful happened during the next couple of years and I was beginning now to look forward to leaving school and going to work so that I could have my own money to spend.

## The Gentle Giant

My mother was a stickler for time keeping and according to age we all had our own times that we should be in by at night. As I was fourteen my time to be in was 10.30 p.m., which I adhered to or suffer the consequences.

One particular night I was waiting at a bus stop in West Green Road for a No. 41 bus which took me to Tottenham Hale, my guitar slung over my shoulder. Suddenly this big American car pulled up and the driver asked if I wanted a lift. Now, my parents had always drummed into me never to accept a lift from a stranger. On closer inspection I thought I recognised the occupants as people I knew and who lived on the same manor. It took five minutes to drive home but instead of dropping me off at my house I was taken to a house in nearby Edith Road.

Everybody got out of the car and entered the house where there seemed to be a party going on. As I knew the house and the people who lived there I had no fear. On entering the living room, I was confronted by about twenty men all wearing trilby hats and sitting around the perimeter of the room. One face stood out to me more than the others, it was none other than The Gentle Giant, as we called him, Tommy Brown, an ex-boxer and occasional minder for the twins Ronnie and Reggie Kray. I often saw him standing outside The White Hart pub in Station Road, where we lived. He would always have time for us kids. I am now thinking how am I going to explain this to my mother?

I had literally been kidnapped and taken to a party to entertain a crowd of hard looking, boozy, street wise, villains. I was to stand in the middle of the room and simply sing and play the guitar. I started off with *My Old Man's a Dustman* by Lonnie Donegan. It went down a treat so now I was relaxed and was playing requests, everyone was singing and having a good time. I was plied with loads of beer and time just seemed to pass me by. I knew it was time to go home when I saw it was 2.45 a.m. but I could have played until it was light. I remember my last song was *Sonny Boy*, recorded by Al Jolson. After this one of the guys took off his hat and passed it around to everyone. I filled my pockets with all this change and walked around the corner to my home.

Not forgetting that in those days there were no mobile phones and most people didn't have house phones either so there was no way of communicating if something cropped up. I gingerly knocked on the door and it seemed an age before it opened. My mother opened the door, she had fallen asleep in the armchair waiting for me to come in. I could see she was only half awake but pretty relieved to see me on the doorstep. She said she would speak to me in the morning as she was going to bed. It was a Saturday morning and none of the family needed to get up early.

On being interrogated, I explained what had happened. I must admit I had enjoyed the experience but still felt sorry for my mother who must have worried herself witless. I avoided the (doughboy) hiding when I told her the events of the previous night. "Tommy Brown", she said, "I'll give him Tommy Brown." I cannot say what happened when she went around to the house but knowing her, there were sparks flying. In those days there was a lot of respect between the families and we all remained friends regardless.

# 8

## Leaving school

My brother Ginger was avidly practicing the guitar and was way ahead of me now. Being six years older than him I was widening my interests in life but still played in the group which we named The Ravens Skiffle Group. Music had now taken over his life and he showed a talent way beyond his years.

It was September 1951 and although leaving school I had no idea of my future out in the big wide world. I had attended this school for the last four years and although having lessons in Science, Metalwork and Woodwork, amongst others, none of them interested me.

There was a company opposite the school in Broad Lane called Gestetner, a large company, which made duplicating machines and employed many Tottenham workers. I suppose having a job on my own doorstep, so to speak, appealed as no expenses would be incurred in bus or train fares. There was so much work about then that nobody had to be unemployed. I applied for and got a job there at £2-03d a week, this also covered two weeks holiday from work per year fully paid. I worked in the press shop stamping out pieces of metal. After working there for eight months and getting my two weeks holiday pay I packed up. It wasn't the job for me.

My eldest brother Sid, who was twenty-eight at the time, was a very good French Polisher and tried to get me to follow in his footsteps. He told me he could get me a job at his firm called Supersuites on the Angel Colony. With the thought of learning a trade especially French Polishing, I accepted. I was told I would be a general dog's body for a while and to see it through. After two years of being a tea boy and burning rubbish I packed that job in too.

I won't go into how many jobs I did and what I learned over the next couple of years, but it all added up to nothing. At least I worked and contributed to my keep.

Leslie, one of my brothers, the black sheep of the family, did not like work in any way, shape or form. He would go to the benefits office, The National Assistance Board, as it was called then. After being asked a few questions he would be paid some money, something in the region of £1-10 shillings (£1.50 in today's money) for one week's benefit. While everyone else in the family, of working age, was paying their way at home, Les was spending his share of the housekeeping money gambling at Haringey or Walthamstow dog tracks. He would come back home begging for another chance saying he had a job to start and that he was going to change his ways. He never did and things came to a head when he broke into, and stole all the money that was in, the gas meter. That did it for mum, he was told to find somewhere else to live and not to come back home again.

On Sundays we would all muck in and help prepare the Sunday dinner. Two of us were shelling peas while another two would be peeling spuds, we were all allocated our own little jobs and we really loved doing it.

It was the one day in the week we were allowed to use the living room, most people in those days didn't use the front room but kept it for best. We had a double leaf table which we extended for Sunday dinner. As there were so many of us we had to take it in shifts to have our meal. The youngest would eat first, followed by the others. Every Saturday it fell to me to go to our butcher, Fisher and Ellis, who had a shop at Tottenham Hale, to get a leg of lamb, it usually cost ten shillings (50p in today's money). When dinner was over, we all mucked in with the washing up and then either went out or listened to the radio.

The Sunday afternoon programme was Educating Archie which was Peter Brough, the ventriloquist and Archie Andrews, who was his puppet. Max Bygraves was the co-starring comedian and the guest singer, on every week, was a very young Julie Andrews. The privileged had a TV and the lesser mortals listened to the wireless or radio.

Every day, our baker left five loaves and the milkman, eight pints of milk. Our indoor entertainment was either playing cards or playing Dogs, this was a game that my eldest brother Sid devised, it was based on greyhound racing and consisted of six players. The board and dogs were made by Sid. The six senior members of the family played the game while the next eldest could stay up and make tea and sandwiches and maybe sit in on the odd game. I was lucky enough to fall into that category. We only played on a Saturday night as no-one had to go to work or school the next morning.

My dad liked to have a bet, as most people did then, and I soon learned how to bet myself. Betting Shops weren't available to punters then, but every locality had a man on the street who would take bets, he was called a bookies runner. Our local runner was a man called Mick Sullivan, who also had a seafood stall at the Hale. The only way we could get results of the greyhound races was to go up to Stamford Hill and get a results sheet. Although Les wasn't living at home we still kept in touch. Jim and Les got together and devised a plan where we could make some money. Les would go to the dog track, which in this case was Haringey, Jim would be in a local phone box at the Hale and wait for Les to phone the result through immediately after the race was run. This gave my dad and my brother time to write out a winning bet and give it to the runner seconds after the race had been run. This worked for some time until he rumbled what we were up to.

Meanwhile our group was doing the odd gig in an East End

pub and we had the pleasure of a visit from the local Pearly King and Queen of Bow. After hearing us play, the Pearly King invited us to perform in his open top bus through the streets of Canvey Island for the Canvey Island Carnival. It really was an enjoyable experience and all the money we collected was for charity.

During this time the Tottenham Royal had become the place to be and I was a regular there on Thursday and Saturday evenings. The Teds would gather and parade in their Edwardian suits and show off their jiving skills to attract the girls. I could cut a rug myself and would take two girls to dance at a time, Maureen and one of her friends. I would often visit Maureen's flat locally and even if she wasn't there I would be welcomed in by her mum. Our relationship was purely platonic, and Maureen would always ask me what I thought of any boyfriend she may have. We were constant companions and I would often take her up to London to see a film.

# 9

## National Service

In March 1955 a brown envelope came through the letterbox with O.H.M.S. on it. My heart sank and I knew what it was before I opened it. Being nineteen now, I really thought that I'd slipped through the net but no such luck. I had to report to a place in Wanstead for a full medical.

I waited two weeks for the result of my army medical and received the news that I had passed. My two brothers Les and Jim both failed their army medical and I was the only family member to do National Service. I found out later that Jimmy played deaf and got away with it and Leslie swallowed small balls of cotton wool and was diagnosed with stomach ulcers. On the 15th of April 1955 I was served with my call up papers and had to make my own way to Wellington Barracks in London where I and other lads were to be picked up in army wagons and driven to Aldershot to await our orders.

On arrival we were taken to the quartermaster's store to get kitted out with our army clothing. Most of us, including myself, had a lovely mop of hair which was cruelly shorn off. I can remember our first orders were to go to our assigned barrack rooms and make our beds. It didn't take us long to find out why. Intake 785, which is what we were, needed to be inoculated against Tetanus.

The jab we were given was called T.A.B. which meant Tetanus Anti Bacteria. It didn't take long to find out why we had to make our beds. Within the next hour I suffered the worst headache I have ever known and felt very feverish.

Because of the effects of this jab we were confined to our beds for forty-eight hours. I thought I was going to die but on the third day the symptoms vanished.

Now we were to learn what the army was all about. There must have been about sixty new recruits and we were split up into five different barrack rooms. We were told how to make our beds properly and lay out our kit for daily inspection.

I guess we all wanted to make an impression and as a team we started to bond straight away with the lads we would be sharing our living quarters with. We were introduced to a certain Sgt. Morrison who would be responsible for us during the coming two weeks. He would show us the ropes and put us in competitive mood to be the best recruits out of the new lads who, like us, had just joined the army. This we achieved after two weeks and for our efforts were allowed a weekend leave. This was a sweetener however, as we were to find out on our return to Blenheim Barracks in Aldershot. The regiment we were in was the R.A.S.C. which was the Royal Army Service Corps. This regiment taught four different trades after three months of basic training.

Now I was in the army and from day one was ticking the days off in my diary. It was a rude awakening and being woken up at 5.30 a.m every morning by some idiot blowing a bugle, having to make my bed, fold my blankets and lay all my kit out on the bed was a pain in the arse. After doing this we all made our way to the canteen where we had breakfast which lasted about an hour. On our return we were told to stand by our beds and await the Sgt. Major's inspection. We all had our bollocking one day or another but gradually learned the ropes and went that extra bit to get it right.

If we thought inspections were hard, we learned a lot more on the square when it came to marching and doing drill with rifles. This is where I had my first run in with my superior and it cost me my independence for fourteen days.

Before being drilled we were always inspected to see if our

cap badge had been polished, our boots sparkled, our trousers pressed, and we all looked immaculate. While being inspected from behind I felt a stick push my hair up and the comment "Get your bloody hair cut." It hurt so much it brought tears to my eyes and without hesitation I swung my arm round and knocked this cocky little git's hat off.

I was immediately marched to the guard room and kept in detention overnight. I was put on a charge and the next morning was marched into the Commanding Officer to explain my behaviour. There was only going to be one outcome. I was found guilty of assaulting a superior ranking corporal and was given fourteen days working in the cookhouse peeling spuds and other general duties. I had only been in the army for two weeks and I thought to myself, bloody hell, you'll never last the two years. I was about to surprise myself.

In whatever leisure time I had I would sit on the grass verge next to the road, which incidentally was called London Road, and plan on making my getaway. Surprisingly enough after three weeks I decided not to fight against it and that it would be much easier to accept the army and get on with it. Lurking in the back of my mind was the feeling that my urge to sing and entertain was overwhelming and would I get a chance to do the one thing I loved doing.

Our six weeks basic training was now coming to an end and the next stage of my army career was just beginning. On completion of the basic training all the recruits that came in on the same day as me were to take part in what's called a Passing Out Parade. We would dress as smart as possible in our army uniform and march to a Military Band. For those whose parents wanted to come and watch it was a very touching moment watching their sons marching and being drilled on the parade ground.

My parents didn't come however but I was not disappointed and felt very proud at what I had achieved. We were all issued with a travel pass and given a week-end leave.

On arriving home, the first thing that entered my mind was how I could get away with a couple of weeks off by going sick. After putting out a few feelers I was recommended to a G.P. who had a surgery in St Anne's Road, I don't remember the name. I visited his surgery on the Monday morning I should have been travelling back to Aldershot.

My information was that for half a crown which was two shillings and sixpence (12 1/2p today) he would sign me off sick for a week with gastro-enteritis. He did exactly this and I reported myself sick and unable to travel. After the week was over, I decided to go back to the doctor and get another certificate for a further week. He told me he could cover me but only for one week at a time, I didn't want to abuse the system, so I made my way back to camp.

Now the basic training had finished we were to be posted to another camp which would be the base for learning a trade which applied to that regiment. I mentioned earlier that the R.A.S.C. taught four trades, these were Butchery, Baking, Driving and Clerical work. We were all issued with a form to fill in stating our preference in order of all four trades. My order of preference was 1. Driving 2. Butcher 3. Baker 4. Clerk. No need to tell you that I was given the duties of a clerk, this was taking army discipline too far, but I realised later that it was to my advantage. I soon learned that my new posting was to be to a large petroleum depot called West Moors which was on the edge of the New Forest in Dorset.

Only six miles from Bournemouth, what a place to be! At least now we would be allowed out of camp in the evening and what's more were allowed to wear our own civilian clothes if we wanted to. It wasn't a bad place on the whole and not as strict as the training camp.

Being as I was now a clerk, I was with several others sent to a typing pool to learn the art of touch typing. It was more like a normal working day now and I was to be employed in the office of the Chief Clerk. It was there that I met a civilian employee by the name of Frank Stone, Frank turned out to be none other than the entertainment manager. We hit it off straight away and he was very interested in what I told him regarding my ambition to be a singer.

Unless it was down to me to do guard duty or switchboard operator I would dress myself up in my civvy togs, catch the bus outside the camp gates and head for the bright lights of Bournemouth. The bus station became the general meeting place for soldiers and the local girls. Not for me though, I was seeking out the clubs and dance halls of which there were quite a few.

One little club I associated myself with was in a basement in the town centre. It was typical of the fifties, small, crowded and very smoky. There was a mixed crowd there of both sexes and a few lads in army uniform. I waited until the group decided they wanted a break then approached the drummer, who I was informed was the group leader. I asked him if it would be possible for me to give a song to which he agreed after a little chat.

On being called up to the stage the crowd quietened, and I was introduced as Ron from Tottenham, a few boos broke the silence but as there were a couple of scousers in the club I expected that anyway. For those of you who were my age group at the time you would remember a song called *The Green Door* which was recorded by Frankie Vaughan, who was a popular singer of that era. I was very happy with the way it went down but even happier at the attention of the opposite sex and one girl in particular. She stood out from the rest with her long, dark, flowing hair and exquisite figure. Even though it is nearly sixty years ago I still remember her name and her address as, Dawn Jessop of The Homestead, Near Winton, Bournemouth, wow what a cracker!

I must go back to my dear friend from home, Maureen, who without fail wrote to me every week and sent me the local rag

The Tottenham Herald so that I could keep in touch with the news going on at home. I was very grateful for this as I didn't have any communication from my family at all.

On my next appearance at the club I was offered a job as a resident vocalist for £10 a session to do three numbers, this took in three sessions a week. Along with my army pay which was roughly £8 per week and my singing job I was earning nearly £40 a week. A very good amount for that time.

## Making a few bob

One of the biggest surprises of my army career was going into the canteen to breakfast one morning and I couldn't believe my eyes when the person serving me was none other than my good mate from back home, Ray Livermore. I thought I was dreaming at first until we got talking and he told me that he was in the Catering Corps and had been posted to my unit as part of his training to be a chef.

It was coming up to Christmas 1955 and Frank Stone was organising a yearly concert which he put on for senior army staff and the lesser mortals, so to speak. After telling him that Ray and I were willing to entertain the rest of the troops we were invited to take part in rehearsals for the concert in which we were to do a double act as Dean Martin & Jerry Lewis. For those of you who remember the Fifties they were a singer and comedy act who did stage shows, made films and were hilariously funny. We also did impersonations of Montgomery and Winston Churchill. To finish the show, we impersonated the top vocalists of the day Frankie Laine, Johnnie Ray, Nat King Cole and Billy Daniels.

It was great to be back doing what I loved but it was just another day in the life of this soldier who hated army life and was marking off every single day of the sixteen months left until my release.

While working in the office of the Chief Clerk, one of my duties, apart from typing daily duty rotas for army personnel, was to order stationery and certain documents. This is where I saw an opportunity to make a few bob for myself. I would order an extra book of travel warrants and sell them on to the lads when they went home on leave. Orders were posted daily stating duties of every individual in camp be it switchboard duties, guard duties or any other. If you had none of these you were free to leave camp every evening providing you signed out and in again when you returned. One of my other duties was operating the switchboard where I took incoming calls for other soldiers who were on duty.

In 1956, through the entertainments organiser, I was informed of a talent competition called the Hampshire Jazz Festival. At that time Bournemouth was in Hampshire, the county boundaries have been moved since then and it is now in Dorset. I decided to enter the competition and through Frank Stone was submitted as a vocalist. I was lucky enough to come through the first and second rounds but had no great expectations of going too much further. Eventually I got to the semi-finals which were held in Christchurch and my song was *Woman in Love* recorded by Frankie Laine, my dream was being realised when I got through to the final. By now Rock 'n' Roll was making its mark in the charts and I was absolutely smitten with this new sound and as soon as I heard *Tutti Frutti* by Little Richard, I knew this was the song I wanted to sing in the final.

It was the big night and the final was to be held in the Civic Hall in Boscombe. I turned up in my army uniform as I had for all the previous rounds. There were eight finalists and I was the last one to sing. I was so happy to get this far that I really wanted to enjoy the moment. I know that I had a lot of support in the theatre but all the finalists were talented in their own field, so I just gave it my best.

The competition was over and we were all paraded on stage. The judge, incidentally, was none other than a top jazz band leader, who was very popular in the fifties, called Harry Gold and his Pieces of Eight which was a traditional jazz band of the era.

The third and second were announced and everybody held their breath, my mind seemed to go numb and then the result was read out. The winner of best vocalist in the 1956 Hampshire Jazz Festival is Private Ron Hepting of the R.A.S.C. Harry Gold presented me with a small oval shaped gold medal. My write up in the Bournemouth Echo said, not a vocalist in the accepted sense but boy what drive and what a gimmick performance, he had everyone rocking. Even today, in 2019, I would love to get hold of that article but because I don't know the exact date of the event I haven't much chance of finding it.

My army life still had to go on and I became employed as an early morning skivvy to a certain Major Taylor. My duties involved getting up at 5.30 a.m. and lighting a stove fire in the Major's office before he started his daily routine. It was also my duty to type everybody's orders for the day which obviously included myself and was surprised to find that I had to dress myself smartly and wait outside the Commanding Officer's quarters at 9 a.m. This procedure only normally happened if you had breached some army regulation. I was marched in, told to stand at ease and then I was given the news. I was to be posted abroad and for that reason was to receive a long week-end leave and to report back to camp for 9.30 a.m. on the following Monday morning. The posting was to Cyprus which at that time wasn't the most popular place to be for a British soldier. However, having never been abroad it was quite an exciting prospect for me.

I reported back to camp after having taken the week-end off and was immediately told to report to the Commanding Officer. This was obviously to receive last minute instructions about my travel arrangements. After going through the rigmarole of being marched into the C.O's office I was told to remove my beret and to stand at ease. I then listened for ten minutes to a talk on what our role was in these far flung reaches of the globe which then culminated in me being told that my posting had been cancelled. No doubt, said the C.O., you are disappointed, well I didn't know there and then whether I was or not. I think the fact that I only had another seven months to go before I completed my two years National Service was a deciding factor in cancelling my deployment.

**Absent without leave**

It was now September 1956 and my unit was to spend two weeks under canvas, camping at Wareham in Dorset. It was the second time I'd been camping so to speak but getting up at 5.30 a.m. in the morning, washing in ice cold water took a bit of getting used to. One tends to make good friends in the army and apart from Ray Livermore I got really pally with a fella who was in fact an amateur boxer from Barking named George Smith. We were free to go anywhere at night providing we signed out and in again on return. This particular evening George, Ray and I went down to Poole harbour to a pub called The Jolly Sailor. Our time to return to camp was midnight. The train station was right opposite the pub.

Apart from keeping my eye on the clock I'd also downed a few pints and didn't really know what time of day or night it was. I found myself the only one left in the bar and realised it was time to go. I stumbled over to the station and was relieved to see a train arriving. Without hesitation I boarded the train knowing that Wareham was only six stations down the line. It won't come as a surprise to anyone when I say that I fell asleep and was woken up by the ticket collector. On showing him my ticket, he told me what I didn't want to hear. "Wareham," he said, "you're now going through the aptly named Woking station and we don't stop until we get to London Waterloo station." Panic immediately set in as I was now classed as absent without leave (A.W.O.L.), this meant another charge and possibly another three weeks in the guardhouse. It must have been about 1.30 a.m. and there were no trains leaving the station to go back until about 5.30 a.m. I had no alternative but to sleep in the waiting area until then. I was notified by the station attendant that I needed to change at a station called Brockenhurst and then get the branch line train to Wareham. I arrived back at camp at about 7.50 a.m. and was pretty relieved regardless of what the outcome might be.

It turned out that my two mates who had been in the pub with me, Ray and George, got back ok and had explained to the powers that be that we had all been having a birthday drink and I had missed the last train back to camp. I was ordered to the C.O.'s tent the same morning and because of my comparatively clean record I was exonerated without charge.

Another person I met whilst doing my bit for Queen and Country was Billy Wells who boxed for the regiment and was a nephew of Bombardier Billy Wells the man who hit the gong in all the J Arthur Rank films. I was now counting the days down to April 1957 and hoping and praying that world affairs would be kind to me in the run up to April 15th when I would be released from National Service.

No such luck however as a crisis broke out in the Suez Canal area of Egypt. I held my breath as other servicemen were conscripted to sail or be flown to the trouble spot. Fortunately for me, I wasn't one of them. On April 15th I became a free man again and looked forward to pursuing my musical career.

# 10

## Work and Play

In 1956 an American artist named Elvis Presley changed the music scene forever, along with Bill Haley's Comets, Little Richard, Fats Domino and Chuck Berry, and my greatest rock star of all time the killer, Jerry Lee Lewis.

During my time away in the army my brother Ginger had devoted his time to learning the guitar and had obviously left me far behind. I suppose I was more interested in singing which worked out quite well between the two of us. I became the rhythm guitarist and vocalist while Ginger played lead guitar. We played in one of our local pubs, The Fountain in West Green Road, Tottenham and also found work in other pubs further afield.

In 1957 my elder brother Jim and I started dabbling on Littlewoods football pools, we did what was called a perm and laid out about fifteen shillings (75p in today's money) a week between us. To hit the jackpot we needed to forecast eight teams to draw at three points each to get twenty-four points. One Saturday we nearly hit the jackpot with twenty-three points. We had to wait until Wednesday to see what we'd won. The top dividend of twenty-four points paid £8,000, 23 paid £350. In the 50's that was a lot of money. I went straight out and bought myself a brand new Lambretta for £125. Now I had my own transport I could go up to Soho to a club called the 2i's in old Compton Street with my guitar slung over my shoulder. I was rubbing shoulders with all the wannabe rock stars of the day, Tommy Steele, Terry Dene, Billy Fury, Marty Wilde and Joe Brown. Those were some of the names that made it, there were plenty of equally talented youngsters who for some reason or other didn't see their dream come true.

One of my disciplines whilst serving in the army was to fold my blankets neatly for morning inspection. I made the mistake of following that trend when I came home. I thought it would impress my mother to see how tidy I was. I soon found out that my expectation was somewhat misplaced. "You're not in the army now," my mother said, "if you want to fucking fold your blankets go back and join the army."

I had a few pounds left over from my pools win and treated my mum to a new coat, I felt it would be nice to do something for her after all she had done for me and the rest of the family. Needless to say she was very pleased with the gift.

My main aim now was to find work. One of the local places to find work was in the local café and in Spooner's at the top of High Cross Road there was always someone looking for people for short term employment and money paid in the hand. Billy Webb was a local person who I knew quite well and he was looking for labourers for a short term period.

In the early fifties local councils in the London area were digging up the old roads to replace them with tarmac roads. These original roads were constructed of wooden blocks to take tracks for trams to run on. Now the trams were being phased out to take more modern means of transport, new roads were replacing old. The blocks were known as tar blocks and became a source of fuel to burn on household fires.

Billy had a contract to collect these blocks and make a stockpile of them in a Hertfordshire field. He would take a truck down to the field in the early morning, bag the blocks up and drive over to Eltham, South London and surrounding boroughs to sell them for five shillings (25p) a sack. It was a good little earner for six months or so but quite a few people jumped on the bandwagon and after about six months the stockpile became depleted and eventually ran out and, like all good things, it came to an end.

I palled up with a fella called Freddie Fallover, who lived in Lorenco Road, known as Little Russia. We discussed taking on a private painting job which was advertised in the Tottenham Herald. The job was in White Hart Lane and was to completely redecorate the outside of a building called St Katherines College. We answered the ad and got the job. Freddie estimated the job and submitted the price. It was accepted and we pooled our resources and hired what equipment we needed from a local builder's yard. The equipment consisted of two extension ladders, two paint kettles, an assortment of paint brushes and a couple of blow lamps to burn off the old paintwork.

After three days we had completed the painting of all the window and door frames and were left with the facia boards and guttering to complete the job. We had already drawn money on completion of work done with three days left to finish the job. The weather had been kind to us and we set about the final stage. The old paintwork would have to be torched and stripped off.

There was a lot of dry growth and old bird's nests under the eaves which needed to be cleared out. The next thing I remember was Freddie telling me to call the Fire Brigade, it's caught fire, he said. Panic set in and I called the Fire Brigade. Within minutes they arrived on the scene and proceeded to put the fire out while Freddie and I remained anonymous. We both watched along with other spectators until the fire was brought under control. As we had kept our identity a secret no one knew who was responsible and we didn't intend anyone should find out.

Me, top row, far left

Me, top row, second from left and below
with mum

Bill (Stanley) in Palestine

Frank

Sissy (Emily)

Barbara, Sylvie, Ray, Brenda, Monty and me

## Ray and Brenda's Wedding

## Ken (Ginger)

Mum    Dad    Barbara    Sylvia

Ray    Monty    Sidney    Jim

Me in full kit on the right

Wally   Bill   Jim   Ray

Beryl

Frank          Jim

Mum having fun

# 11

## Meeting the parents

Visiting the local labour exchange or as it's known now the Job Centre, Ginger and I were offered jobs as labourers at a company in Edmonton called The Fleetway, we were accepted and were told to start on Monday morning. We had no idea what the work would involve but when it was explained to us, we agreed to take the job. It was a company that made carpet cleaners and lawn mowers and was a subsidiary of Qualcast. We adapted quite well and came to like it.

We got to hear that one of the girls was having a house party for her eighteenth birthday. There was a pretty girl who worked in a different department to me that had caught my eye and I made a point of passing her workbench two to three times a day just to see her.

All the fellas that the birthday girl knew were invited and had to bring a female friend. Tickets were then printed with the couple's names on to be shown on arrival. My brother and I both arranged to take two girls and I was over the moon when the young lady I'd asked consented to go. She was of course the girl I passed by every day on my way to the loo.

We decided to take our guitars to provide extra entertainment. I established that the girl my brother was taking was named Jean and my date was called Ruby. We had a wonderful time until gradually people started to dwindle and it was time to call it a day. Ruby didn't live too far away and I walked her home to where she lived in St Mary's Gardens,

Edmonton. We talked for a while and when she said she had to go in, I asked her if she minded if I kissed her goodnight, she said she didn't mind and so started the romance that turned my whole world around.

I left her and started my long walk home to Tottenham Hale. It took over one and half hours to get home, but it was so worth it. Of course, now I had my own key I didn't have to worry about what time I got in. It was now Sunday and Monday couldn't come soon enough for me to see her again. For us to keep in contact we would arrange at work where we could meet each other as neither of us had a house phone.

Meanwhile, Ginger and I were still playing in pubs and working mens' clubs although we had disbanded the group and were playing as a duo. I saw Ruby as much as I could and now I had my scooter it would only take me fifteen minutes to get home. I learned from her that her father wasn't too keen on me after my first meeting with her parents. The reason though wasn't very clear to me. The weeks and months passed by and our relationship grew day by day. I had now become a regular visitor to her home and seemed to have won over her father.

One evening while we were all sitting watching TV Ruby's father jumped up out of his armchair, switched on the lights and said he needed to have a chat with me. We all wondered what the hell was happening. He was a foreman at the company he worked for and had been there for twenty-eight years and I could only imagine that, being a common labourer and having a poorer background, I really wasn't considered good enough for his daughter. Apparently, it all boiled down to me and he accused me of leading his daughter, as he put it, up the garden path. Obviously, parents are very protective of their children but what he said couldn't have been further from the truth. At that time, I was twenty-two and Ruby was eighteen. We had discussed getting married and our minds were made up, that's what we wanted. Her father told her that she was forbidden to see me. This was never going to work as we'd fallen in love with each other. My only fear was that to keep the peace at home she would be persuaded to break off the relationship.

Eventually she wrote to me saying that her father wasn't prepared to accept me as a member of the family and that she didn't want to see me again. I was totally distraught and didn't know what to do. In my desperation, although I had never done it before, I spoke to my mother and showed her the letter. Her words to me were very comforting, she said, reading between the lines you need to be strong and if it is meant to be it will be. I told Ruby that if I spoke to her father and explained my true feelings and intentions there was a chance that he would see that I was genuine and wanted to marry his daughter. He wouldn't hear of it and to be honest instead of driving a wedge between us it brought us closer together.

Meanwhile, through the New Musical Express I got to find out that my top Rock 'n' Roll star was about to tour the United Kingdom and would be appearing at the Regal Cinema in Edmonton on 24th May 1958. Jerry Lee Lewis was doing a show at this venue and at all costs I had to get tickets for Ruby and I. I couldn't miss this opportunity knowing that it may never come around again.

It was all I expected it to be on the night but obviously you had to be a fan to like it. During his tour it came to light that he had married his thirteen year old cousin Myra, the press crucified him and for his sins, his tour was cut short and his career ended in tatters. Whatever he did with his private life did not affect me, the one thing that affected me and the rest of his fans was to see his disappearance from the top 50 musical charts. Being a fan, I bought his top chart hits including *Whole Lotta Shakin'*, *Great Balls of Fire*, *Sweet Little Sixteen*, *Rockin' at the High School Hop* and *You Win Again*. I know that somewhere in America he is still performing in clubs and in cabaret and I, despite what the press and others may say, admire him and play his music regardless. Long live J.L.Lewis.

# 12

## Married life

In January of 1959 Ruby and I found out that we were going to be parents. I now had the unenviable task of confronting her parents with the news. On the Sunday evening in question myself, Ruby and her parents were watching The Black and White Minstrel Show on TV when I plucked up courage to tell them. It was about 8.30 p.m. and I got up from the settee, switched on the lights and said, "I have something to tell you." My heart was pounding like a drum but I had no hesitation in saying that Ruby was pregnant. The silence was deafening and then her mother said, "What did I say Bill, I knew this would happen." I found her mother more understanding and she gave Ruby a cuddle and said, "Let's have a talk." Her father's first words were "Do you intend to marry her." I told him that I did and not because she was pregnant but because she was pregnant and that I loved her.

On a snowy, very cold, February 21$^{st}$ 1959 Ruby and I were married at Tottenham Registry Office. No one turned up from her family or mine except my closest brother Ginger, who was my sole witness. On finding out that Ruby was pregnant in January it gave me a chance to find a flat to move into in Summerhill Road, off West Green Road in Tottenham.

In 1959 I took my eldest brother Sid to see the Epsom Derby. It took me ninety minutes on the Lambretta with Sid on the back. We had a great day even though we came home skint. We did however see Liz Taylor at the races with her then husband Michael Wilding.

This gave me the idea to take the in-laws to see the Derby. I approached them with trepidation but was pleasantly surprised when they accepted my offer and plans were set for the big day. They had never been to a race-track before but I could see they were out to enjoy themselves which made for a wonderful family day out. The race was won by Royal Palace, unfortunately none of us had backed it.

It was round about this time that my mum was diagnosed with breast cancer and would need to undergo a double mastectomy at the Prince of Wales Hospital in Tottenham. I didn't have a full time job around that time and I would take mum on the back of the scooter to the hospital for her appointments to have radium treatment. After treatment mum was now in remission and out of danger of the disease spreading. There was a side effect however which she would have to live with for the rest of her life. Her left arm swelled up to twice it's normal size for which she had to do exercises. Mum coped with it admirably, still had her bottle of Mackeson and the odd cigarette.

Six months later I moved into the flat with Ruby. In early Oct 1959 Ruby was taken into a nursing home known as The Towers in The Bishops' Avenue, Hampstead, known as Millionaires Row. The patron of the nursing home was Gracie Fields, singer and forces entertainer during the war.

**Then there were three**

On the 8th Oct a General Election was taking place, I remember sitting up all evening listening to the results on the radio. I must have fallen asleep and I didn't wake up till 7 a.m. I immediately got dressed and went downstairs where there was a wall phone in the hallway. I rang the nursing home and was informed that my wife had given birth to our daughter at 3.30 a.m. on the 9th Oct 1959. It was the most emotional feeling I'd ever had in my entire life and I couldn't wait to see them. I wanted the world to know how happy I was. In all, Ruby was confined for ten days before she was allowed to bring the baby home.

Meanwhile I had obtained a top of the range Swallow pram on hire purchase and my friend Maureen had bought an exquisite baby shawl. I paraded my daughter up and down Tottenham High Road in her new pram and soaked up the adoration of all my friends. We named her Dawn Rose.

It was only natural that Ruby wanted to show the baby off to her family and I'm glad to say that their support was unstinting. I was amazed when her father asked her if the three of us wanted to come and live with them as they had a spare room. I had no problem accepting as our own flat was pretty dire and lacked heating. We gave the landlord the obligatory one month notice before vacating the premises. During the second week of that month I had a surprise visit from my elder brother Les, he told me he had nowhere to stay and was living rough. After speaking to Ruby, we agreed to let him stay for one night and sleep on the floor with a couple of cushions, that's the best we could do. On waking in the morning, I found that he had gone and so was my brand new overcoat that I had bought a month earlier.

The first thing to do now was to put my name down on the local housing list in Edmonton in anticipation of acquiring a council house of our own.

Ginger had got a job as a resident musician in an East End pub called The Market House in London Fields. There we met an old friend, Roy Young, who used to entertain in The Fountain pub in West Green Road, he was a pianist and vocalist and he was the nearest thing I'd ever heard to Little Richard. He told us that if we had been born in America, we'd have made it by now. The last I heard of Roy he became the keyboard player for a group called Cliff Bennett and the Rebel Rousers. There were a lot of characters around in the music business at that time and one of them was a singing cowboy called Tex. He was a regular visitor to the Market House with his horse, his horse would come in with him and Tex would do a couple of country and western songs.

## A new arrival and a cup final

My time now was taken up by my daughter and the only work I did musically was to entertain socially, now and again, in the various pubs I visited. Nothing much happened in 1960 except for the fact that we had moved in with Ruby's parents and life went on as it should. Then in August of that year Ruby told me she was pregnant. We had discussed a family and I was overjoyed when she told me the news. We now had a strong case for getting a council place of our own, where it would be we didn't know.

On Saturday, April 15th 1961, while I was twiddling my thumbs downstairs Ruby was giving birth to a son, our second child, who we named Kevin. I was eventually told by the midwife that I could go upstairs and see my wife and our newborn son. It was very emotional and after a while I left, allowing her family to make a fuss.

In the world of football, my second passion, Tottenham Hotspur were having a great season and, apart from looking assured of winning the first division championship, had now reached the semi-final of the FA Cup and were drawn to play Burnley at a neutral ground, on this occasion the Villa Park ground. They had already beaten Aston Villa in a previous round and now needed to win to play in the final at Wembley Stadium. A group of local Spurs fans organised a coach party and there was no way I was going to miss out on this occasion. As this momentous event took place all those years ago I can only tell you that the final score was 3-1 to Spurs, although I do remember that Ray Pointer scored for Burnley and Bobby Smith, the England centre forward, scored for Spurs. The outcome of this was that Spurs would play Leicester City in the FA cup final at Wembley in May of 1961 for the honour of becoming the first team in the 20th century to win the league and cup double.

I wasn't lucky enough to get a ticket for the final but watched the game on national TV. Kevin was four weeks old and I'm sure was one of the youngest spurs supporters on the day of the match. I won't bore you with lots of details but when Bobby Smith scored a goal in the second half the roof came off the stadium, then some time later Terry Dyson headed in the second goal and history was made. Spurs won 2-0.

**'Pie and Mash'**

I still had my prize possession, the guitar that I bought for £5 from the Swap Shop in West Green Road, some years earlier. One morning I remember Ruby and I having a bit of a barney before I left for work and thought no more of it. When I came home I was confronted with the remains of my guitar which had been smashed to pieces. There were no words to express my feelings, I broke down and cried.

However, In the September of that year on my twenty-fifth birthday I left for work. I was now working for an engineering company in Tramway Avenue and training to be a fully-fledged machine setter. Ruby's brother, Ken had got me the job and I had been there about a year. On arriving home after work I was greeted by Ruby with the most beautiful birthday present I could ever wish for. There lying on the bed was a brand new electric guitar and amplifier. I was emotionally overwhelmed and treated Ruby to a night out at the Market House where my brother, Ginger, was playing. Fortunately, friends provided transport for us so we could celebrate and have a few bevvies. We stopped to have a meal in an Indian restaurant in Stoke Newington, on our way home, and that was the first and the last Indian meal I ever had. Give me Pie and Mash any day of the week.

Ruby had packed up work to become a full time mum and because we lived with her parents, they would babysit for us which would allow us to have some social life. We would go up to London to see a show or maybe a concert or visit a couple of local pubs where I would do what I love best, entertaining. Johnny Mathis was our favourite singer and entertainer and whenever he was on, we went to see him perform. His shows at the Prince of Wales Theatre in London were sell outs, he was amazing.

It was around this time in 1962 that we received a letter from the local council offering us a three bedroom house in Cheshunt. Now, for me, Cheshunt was the edge of the world as we knew it. Strangely enough everything turned around there and to venture beyond London was a new experience. We couldn't wait to see our house and we were not to be disappointed. It was set in typical green Hertfordshire countryside with a green playing area for the children and a boating and fishing lake beyond the road, which was called Brookfield Lane, a very different road today! Our house was in the aptly named, Lakeside Road. The best was yet to come. 100 yards down Brookfield Lane was the Spurs training ground and 200 yards in the opposite direction was the pub that became my local, The White Horse.

**A new start and a new arrival**

This was so different to living in the suburbs of London, it's amazing what a difference it makes to your outlook on life when moving to the open spaces of the countryside. We would take the children for long walks down country lanes and the surrounding areas of Wormley, Turnford and Hoddesdon.

Our first priority was to get them enrolled in the local nursery school, Flamstead End. I was still travelling daily back to Ponders End where I worked but my thoughts turned to getting a job locally in Cheshunt. I had bought myself a moped for travelling but now seriously thought about buying a second-hand car not only for work but for leisure. It didn't take long to get a job as there were housing estates being built all around, two in Cheshunt, the Rosedale Estate and Russells Ride and also Ninefields in Honey Lane, Waltham Abbey. Although it meant disappointing my brother in law and equally my employers, I terminated my job at Ponders End and started my new career as a painter and decorator on the Rosedale Estate. I was self-employed and as long as I was paying a weekly insurance stamp and employing a Chartered Accountant to work out my tax returns, I was within the law.

However, the money in my hand every week tempted me to overlook what was legal and what wasn't and I soon fell into bad habits with HM Inspector of Taxes and my national insurance contributions. This obviously would affect me later on in life with my state pension but at the time I wasn't too bothered, it was a long way off.

I got myself an evening job playing guitar with a jazz band in a local pub called The Old English Gentleman. Old habits die hard. Now it was time to count my blessings, concentrate on raising my family and put my music second, so to speak.

My two children were enrolled in Flamstead End School some fifteen minute walk from the house. I had the security of a good job and now with a car was able to take the family out on Sunday trips to various locations in Hertfordshire and Essex. One such trip was to Stansted airport where we would see the occasional plane. It wasn't a fully commercial airport at that time, nevertheless, it was exciting for the children.

January 1967 and Ruby was expecting our third child. I couldn't wait to give the good news to her parents but most of all to let her father see how happy we were and to dispel any misgivings that he had about our relationship when we first met. Kevin and Dawn at this time were getting excited about the arrival of a new addition to the family which by now was only twelve weeks away. Kevin was now a regular visitor to the Spurs training ground so I decided to take him to see his first game at White Hart Lane where Spurs were at home to West Ham Utd. Kevin was only six years old and I took him in the enclosure paying one shilling and sixpence and lifted him over the perimeter fence where he sat and watched the game with the likes of Jimmy Greaves, Alan Gilzean and Bobby Moore on show.

On Thursday, 14th September of 1967 the new addition to the family arrived. The midwife had been called and while I waited downstairs Ruby was giving birth to our son, who we named, Michael. Out of the blue, I was summoned to the bedroom by the midwife. I gingerly made my way upstairs and was greeted with the words, Mr Hepting have you got a 3/8 ths spanner? I had one in my tool-box and with some trepidation handed it to the midwife to do whatever she needed to do. My interest was aroused now and I watched as she adjusted a nut on the gas and air bottle. I stayed to witness the birth and this was the most emotional moment of my entire life. It was an experience I shall never forget and I had assisted in more ways than one. Ruby and the baby were well and he was the spitting image of his dad. We decided then we were happy with three children.

Kevin for some reason or other took a fancy to collecting birds eggs, and as a result, there were a few occasions when I had to drive him to the local cottage hospital as he'd injured himself when falling out of the odd tree. He built up quite an interesting collection, I'm still not sure whether it was illegal or not back then but it didn't last all that long.

I had taken a keen interest in fishing at his age and decided to take him with me one Sunday to, more or less, a local spot on the River Lea at Dobbs Weir. We took a flask of tea and some sandwiches and I let him use my rod to try it himself. I'm pleased to say he was very keen and so I bought him his own rod and all the accessories, he took to it like a duck to water. Every other Sunday that I wasn't working I would set the alarm for 4 a.m. and we would go down to Dobbs Weir, fish until midday, weather permitting, and get home in time for Sunday dinner.

Because people got to know I played guitar we had regular house parties at No. 3 Lakeside Road and in order to get to know the locals we had open house to all who wanted to join in. Through this we became great friends with a couple who lived across in Whitefields Road named Ronnie Jones and his wife Christine. They were originally from Edmonton, as was Ruby. Another two who attended our parties were local travellers, Peter Miles, a coalman, nicknamed Milo and Brian Gumble whose nickname was Mothball. They became minders at all our parties but thankfully nothing went off.

When Dawn and Kevin left junior school they were enrolled in Riversmead School just down the road. This, incidentally, was the school Cliff Richard attended as a pupil as he formerly lived in Cheshunt and was known to visit the school occasionally after he became famous. Dawn had inherited musical attributes too and had a good singing voice, she loved all the music of her parents era as well as that of her own musical era.

We decided to add a couple of pets to the family, one an Alsatian and the other a tabby kitten which the children named Lulu. It was a most extraordinary kitten as it had an extra toe on both front legs which resembled a boxing glove. We named the dog Tara. Long before Cheshunt Golf Club was established the land was all open with a massive orchard which was open to the public. We would take Tara there and slip her lead so she could run as she pleased.

Whenever we had one of our parties we always got aggro from our next door neighbour, Ted. He was always told in advance when we would be having a party but would always knock on the front door halfway through proceedings whereby he was invited in to join us.

Life in general seemed to be going along as it should and we were grabbing the odd holiday now and then, nothing spectacular, maybe Gt Yarmouth or Camber Sands, but the kids loved it. There I had a chance to enter the holiday talent competition which I really enjoyed.

By the same token I was really glad to get back to work after having been off because of my accident. The accident happened while working on a housing estate in Waltham Abbey, my ladder slipped and while coming down face first, threw my arms out to protect my face and smashed my elbow on the icy concrete path. I was taken by car to St Margaret's Hospital in Epping only to find that I had shattered the ball joint in my elbow. To cut a long story short, I was side lined for three months while being treated for my mishap at the North Middlesex Hospital in Edmonton.

In the early seventies, I remember one particular party we had at our home, Tara the Alsatian had run out through the front door and straight into the path of an oncoming car, sadly she was fatally injured and the kids were beside themselves with grief. This happened about a week before Christmas.

Christmas time was very special for the kids. I would get Dawn and Kevin to write out their letters for Father Christmas and when there was no fire we would all sit in front of the fireplace. I would throw their letters up the chimney and because there was a strong up draught the notes disappeared which was all very exciting for them as this meant that Father Christmas had accepted them.

This particular Christmas lunchtime I had arranged to meet Milo in the White Horse. We had our bevy and the bell went for last orders as pubs then were open at lunchtime from 12 till 2 p.m. As I was getting ready to walk home, Milo gave me something wrapped in a blanket. It was the cutest little Alsatian puppy I have ever seen. The children were thrilled all of which added to the most wonderful Christmas of all time.

Although we were not well off we were very happy, or so I thought, there seemed nothing to suggest otherwise until my whole world fell apart.

*My children and friends' children*

# 13

## Homeless

This was a chapter in my life that I don't want to re-live but will briefly relate what happened. After fourteen years of marriage, my wife told me that she was pregnant, that she'd had an affair and that the baby wasn't mine. At first I found this situation surreal and my solution was to accept this baby and to rear the child as my own. I didn't want to lose my wife and this was my way of telling her that no matter what, I still loved her and wanted her in my life. I told her I was prepared to overlook what she'd done and carry on our life as normal. I'm not ashamed to say I sat up night after night begging and pleading with her not to break up the family until finally she said, "I'm sorry, I don't love you." Within several days of that she left the family home and took up residence with a lady friend who also lived on the estate.

Everything happened so quickly I didn't know which way to turn. I felt betrayed, not only by my wife but by the person who had accommodated her who I thought to be a good friend of the family. I must say here and now that Ruby had asked me many times and mentioned that she would like to do a part time job perhaps in the evenings to give her a break from the kids and to be a bit more independent. For some reason this made me feel insecure but eventually I gave in and said it would be OK. It doesn't take a genius to work out what happened then.

I wanted and needed to keep my family together so I applied to the County Court for a custody order, thankfully this was granted to me. I immediately organised a plan for myself and the two older children to help me run the house, their contribution was a revelation even though they were fourteen and twelve at the time.

I couldn't understand why, out of the blue, I had a visit from the welfare people. On asking the problem I was told that a certain person had phoned them and reported me for neglect of the home and the children. This was totally untrue and I, along with the children, were subjected to an enquiry and a complete examination of the children's health and the cleanliness of the home which, on both counts, were deemed to be 100%. I was astounded to learn that my wife was the informant. This was obviously the act of a desperate woman to get back into the house.

It wasn't too long before her next move and one that would be decisive in the complete break-up of the family of which I had tried so desperately to keep together. I had not left any instructions with Dawn or Kevin not to open the door to anyone who happened to knock, this proved to be a great oversight on my part. One afternoon while I was at work, and Ruby knew I wouldn't be home, she came round and knocked on the door. My daughter opened the door and unwittingly let her mother into the house. This was the last thing I wanted unless she wanted to work something out between us.

Unfortunately this wasn't the case and I was left to make a decision that I thought would be best for the family. That decision was made for the sake of my children. I could not let them grow up in an atmosphere of hate, intimidation and fear. I got them all together and told them that because of the situation I would sit down with my family for Sunday dinner and I would be leaving afterwards. This I did. Kevin who was twelve at the time said, "Dad, can I come with you." I left him, crying, following me down the path at the front of the house. I wanted to turn round but did not. I so wanted Ruby to say don't go, but she didn't and as I walked away my heart was breaking and all the time thinking, God don't let this happen.

I remember just getting into my car and driving off not knowing where I was going or what I was going to do. I found it hard to move too far away from my family and reality struck when night fell and the sudden realisation that I was homeless and I was destined to spend the coming days and nights living and sleeping in my car. I was fortunate enough to have a job but my life was in tatters.

## Homeless

I literally became a vagrant and was looking over both shoulders for a friend. It took four weeks living in my car before a friend of the family said I could stay with them until I could find myself a place to live. I accepted readily but found it difficult to live in a house where the children were young adults and I was taking up their space. I discussed this with Mary, who was putting me up, and it wasn't too long before she arranged for me to stay at her sister in law's place who incidentally also had a family but were a lot younger than Mary's family. The couple who took me in were Mary's brother John and his wife Janet, who was a northerner from Sheffield. They had three young children, Cresta, Tracey and Sean.

I was at a stage in my life where children were an important part of me and I would sit for hours with the three of them and read to them and entertain them as if they were my own. Janet loved a drink and especially a drop of barley wine, so each Friday when I finished work and had a few shekels in the bin I would drop into the off-licence and treat her as a thank you. I missed my children so much it was heart breaking. There was no access agreed between me and Ruby so I didn't get to see my kids at all.

While walking down the High Street one day I was so pleased to bump into Kevin and he came back to the house with me and from there we arranged that, now he knew where I was living, he would come round to see me whenever he could.

On certain weekends a party would be suggested where I was living and I had no hesitation in agreeing and supplying the music. On one particular occasion I arranged a party where I would play some party records and with a few background sounds I'd recorded on cassette made it sound like we were in a pub. With me playing the guitar and people clinking glasses, asking for cigarettes and crisps, ordering drinks and doors being opened and shut it really sounded quite authentic.

I was as happy as Larry when on Christmas Eve there was a knock on the door and there stood Kevin. It was an emotional moment and I gave him a big hug. He then handed me a cigar and said, "Happy Christmas Dad." my tears were visible to all but at that moment I didn't give a damn. He didn't stay too long but that was my Christmas present.

Whilst living with Janet I received a letter from Ruby's solicitor containing the divorce papers. I didn't contest the divorce and it was granted to her under title of, Irretrievable breakdown because of unreasonable behaviour. That's right, Ruby had not only committed adultery but had become pregnant in the process. We both agreed that no maintenance would be forthcoming which was countersigned by her solicitor. In a divorce court I would have had the law on my side but I wasn't prepared to see my children suffer in a degrading contest of what's his and hers which would be dragged out in a court of law.

Throughout the fourteen years we were married I was never unfaithful even though I was accused of being so several times. At that time, several months after leaving home I was finding it very difficult to cope with the absence of my children and having to live with other people's families. It had been two months now since moving in with Janet and John and because of the somewhat cooling atmosphere I decided to look elsewhere for accommodation. However, I will say that I was more than grateful to them for what they did for me.

I immediately acquired a single room less than half a mile away in Cheshunt High Street. My stay there was a short one as there were too many restrictions. I now had two part time jobs locally and for several reasons wanted to remain in the locality. My first priority though was to find somewhere to live. I didn't now have my own vehicle but one of my part time jobs was as an office window cleaner and my employer supplied me with a company van which was a great asset.

My mother still lived in Tottenham in a three bedroom house in High Cross Road so I decided to ask her if she could put me up until I could find a one bedroom flat in Cheshunt. She agreed and said there were certain rules I had to follow.

By this time I had lost my family, my home and was about to lose my job. I was at my lowest ebb and decided to visit my G.P. who immediately prescribed Valium. I was now drinking heavily, smoking and topping up with prescription tablets every day.

I found that when I got to my mum's, my youngest brother, Monty was also living there after things hadn't worked out in his marriage. It was strange being back at my mum's and there were certain house rules that she laid down which I found hard to come to terms with but obviously had to adhere to. I wasn't allowed a front door key and had to be in by a certain time or I would be locked out. That time was 11 p.m. and after I had been locked out several times I decided enough is enough and I would have to move on. I guess Monty being the youngest and mum's pet he could do no wrong and I felt like an intruder. I paid my way up to the day I left but didn't say I was leaving. During all this turmoil I heard from my sister, Barbara, that Ginger had met a Greek girl, Roula, while he was working in Athens entertaining the American Forces at their NCO club, and had got married on February 20th 1972. Ironically, I had got married on Feb 21st 1959, some coincidence.

Fortunately, I was cleaning some offices in West Green Road and had a key to let myself in. I slept on these premises for about a month until I got another job in Cheshunt. I now had three part time jobs. One was in a local betting shop, the second was doing a window and office cleaning round for a local company and third was selling newspapers etc. on a news stand for a local newsagent at Theobalds Grove train station. It was now 1976 and because I was still living rough I was thankful for the summer of that year which was very hot and living in my van was made more tolerable.

With the three jobs I must have been working sixteen hours a day and drinking another four which, unless I wanted to kill myself, was definitely not sustainable. With the news stand I found that I could do deals with my customers which would benefit both parties. One particular customer I got to know worked up town for the after shave company, Aramis. So for the magazine, Cosmopolitan and 20 Silk Cut fags on a Monday I would get a £12 bottle of Aramis. I met some lovely young ladies on the stall and would arrange out of hours to take them over to the Coach and Horses pub, opposite the station, for a social drink or a meal and listen to their tales of woe and offer a shoulder to cry on.

One particular customer whose name was Maureen would, time allowing, have a chat with me and after listening to my story said that she had a spare room and was looking for a lodger. When she told me where she lived I had no hesitation in accepting. There was a condition however. She travelled quite a lot and wanted me to look after her cat while she was away. I accepted without question. She lived in Cecil Road, more or less opposite the station which was ideal for me. After I'd been there about four weeks she told me that she was going on holiday to Italy and she would leave me the money to buy the cat food while she was away. She would be away three weeks and £20 should cover the expenses. She wasn't kidding, I had to go to the local fish & chip shop and buy coley every day, 'kin ell' the cat was eating better than me. Mind you, she had a cocktail cabinet with some classy wine in it so I had a little dabble after coming in from the Temple Bar pub which became my local and was just round the corner.

It was during this period that I had to make up my mind which way my life was going. I was still drinking heavily and topping up with Valium. I got very friendly with a group of travellers in the pub and if I played the guitar they would ply me with drinks all night. One was Bingo and his wife Minnie who I got to know quite well. On Derby day, Minnie would be at the station with an array of clothes pegs and selling a tip for the big race.

It was while working on the stand that I met Tony Flanagan. We got on really well and went for a few drinks together in several local pubs. He originally came from the Caledonia Road, well known as the *Cally*, and was reputed to be a bit of a scoundrel. One day, knowing I had a van he asked me if I could do him a favour and drive him up to his sister's house in East London. No questions asked, I took him up there and to cut a long story short he came back with a handful of snooker cues. I took him back to the George pub at the Old Pond in Cheshunt where he was well known. He knocked them out pretty cheaply and after that we became very good friends. Incidentally, he gave me one of the cues as I played a lot of pool at that time.

On one particular night I was on a bender in The Castle pub in Waltham Cross and needed to go to the gents. On the wall in the toilet there was a full length mirror, I stopped to take a look at myself and was shocked at the pitiful sight I saw in front of me. Was this wreck of a human being really me and if so what if anything could I do about it? I cut out the Valium and became less liberal with my drinking habits and made every effort to get back on course in the real world. Thankfully, normality returned to my everyday life but the heartache and trauma of the break-up of my family and marriage would stay with me for a very long time.

## Mum  Ginger  Roula  George  Despina

## Ginger and Roula

# 14

## Fresh Starts

Now there was a pattern to my life, a routine, I had got out of that downward spiral and really wanted to shake off this mantle of self-destruction and self-pity. The moment I felt inspired was when Dawn told me she was getting married. Her husband to be, Kim, was Dawn's first real true love and I know I had frightened a few suitors away in happier times when we lived together. I was still residing in Cecil Road and the arrangements were for me to be picked up from that address and be taken to her best friend, Paula's house in Franklin Ave, just round the corner from St Mary's Church in Churchgate. I had already acquired the services of a young lady hairdresser and surprised everybody with my Afro haircut. We drove the three or four hundred yards to the church and after greeting everybody, took our places. I was absolutely horrified to notice her mother's absence. The time came and I had a tear in my eye as my daughter held my arm as we walked down the aisle. I shall never forget the moment my foot got tangled in the train of her wedding dress and I lurched forward, no damage was done however and reverential order was restored. The date is etched in my memory, Saturday, 19th Aug 1978, the one shining star in a very dark sky.

### Sanity restored

The owner of the newsagent that I worked for knew that I was living in digs but said that she had a plan that might work with the local council if I was willing to try it out. She would be

# My daughter Dawn

## Dawn on her wedding day with her proud dad

be willing, if needed, to tell the council officer that I was homeless and was sleeping on the premises, with her permission, after the shop had been closed. She did this and also told them that I was a trustworthy employee but the situation could only be temporary as my presence on the site had triggered the burglar alarm system when I went to the toilet. Within days she received a letter from the council inviting me to an interview with the housing association.

In November 1978 I turned up for the interview looking like a vagrant with a runny nose, holes in my socks and a bedraggled afro, I must have looked like something the cat had dragged in. I left that building none the wiser but was told I would be notified of their decision. It took four days for the shopkeeper to tell me that I needed to go back to the council and that there was a chance of me acquiring a council bedsit in the Cheshunt area.

My sanity was restored when I was asked if I knew Grove House and was given the keys to a bedsit on the 2nd floor of what turned out to be a forty flat tower block. My only asset was a bar stool from the Temple Bar which took pride of place in my own home. I couldn't thank my employer enough and promised to decorate her flat free of charge which was also in a tower block at St Cyprians Court on the Holdbrook Estate. She was quite happy for me to re-paint and paper a couple of rooms.

My job at the station lasted another three years until my employer sold out and I had to move on. In some ways this came as a welcome break as, after working eighteen hours a day, I could get back to some sort of normality doing two jobs and fourteen hours a day.

I began to pick up the threads of where I left off in my life and started to re-visit the White Horse, my ex local. It was on one of these visits that I made the acquaintance of a young lady who, when I first saw her, seemed to have the world on her shoulders. I ventured to ask if I could join her and was surprised when she willingly invited me to sit at her table. She was very pretty, aged about thirty-five and seemed to be in need of a kindly word.

This suited my purpose too as we could be lonely together. Her name was Jacqueline and she was going through a bad time with divorce proceedings. Over the coming weeks we helped each other to see that there is a good side to life and a friend in need is a friend indeed, so the saying goes. Not only was she suffering mental pain but she had to endure osteoarthritis which had taken over her body. She was so very independent and would rear up if I tried to assist her across the road. She had a very good job as a receptionist in an opticians called Junipers whose premises were at the Old Pond in Cheshunt, today it's known as the Eye Emporium.

Jacqueline was very high on medication for her condition and always carried antibiotics with her. She confided in me and told me that her bones were literally, slowly but surely melting. She lived in a flat above Jennings the Bookmaker, opposite The Plough, Flamstead End.

Over the next year we became quite intimate friends and although I didn't show it I felt very sorry for her. Jacqueline confided in me and no way could I ever betray that trust. She was denied all the treasures of life that women should have. Her dearest wish in life was to have a child and that if it were possible she wanted me to be the father. This desire was never to be as she had it on good authority that she could never have children. We had formed a bond between us as she was estranged from her husband. She loved a drink and most evenings could be found sitting on a bar stool in the Plough pub opposite her flat. She was a very pretty lady and would attract an army of admirers because she loved company.

I guess, as we all think it helps, she would drink to drown her sorrows and to numb the constant pain she was in because of her condition. One summer's evening I was alone in my flat when my phone rang. It was Jacqueline, ringing me from the

Plough, she asked me to come to the pub as there were people all around her and they had guns and were threatening to break into her flat. Something didn't sound right to me so I got a bus up to the pub and was there in thirty minutes. I looked in the saloon bar which is where she would be and couldn't see her.

My heart was jumping out of my chest and I asked one of the lads had he seen her. I went completely numb when he told me that she had left in an ambulance. I was at a loss to know what to do so after asking what had happened I made my way home. The story I was told was that she had been drinking large brandies and taking her medication with alcohol and had started to hallucinate, hence the gunmen. I left a message with the landlord of the pub to inform me if and when there was any news. I was notified three hours later that she was dead as a result of overdosing while under the influence of alcohol. I truly believe that it wasn't meant and that it was a horrible accident and I felt so guilty that I hadn't been able to get to the pub in time. Jacqueline was only thirty-six years old, what a dreadful waste of a lovely young lady's life.

It was six months later that I had a letter from a local solicitor asking if I knew the deceased as they would like to speak to me. I arranged to go to their offices at Cheshunt Pond and they showed me a will that she had started to write naming me as beneficiary to her flat but because the will was never finished, legally it was invalid but it was their duty to notify me.

**Finally, a home of my own**

It took me a couple of years to get my flat resembling a place to live and it appeared that I was one of the youngest tenants in the block. The property called, Grove House, consisted of three main buildings. The Tower Block, the warden controlled block and the maisonettes. Those elderly tenants in the block who were able to look after themselves didn't need a carer but those who were less capable were

# Jacqueline

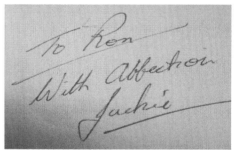

transferred to the warden controlled block where their needs were taken care of. It was more or less a hospice. I would check on several O.A.P's who I got to know and go to the shops for them and generally help them out with different things. Slowly but surely I was settling down to a routine and a way of life that I found very hard to come to terms with.

At forty-four years old I felt completely lost. I had no, what I would call, friends, maybe a few acquaintances and drinking buddies. I decided to try and get back into circulation by going back to all my old haunts notably the White Horse which was my original local. I was warmly welcomed back by the younger generation who grew up on the estate with Dawn and Kevin and they showed me a lot of respect. I wondered what the powers above have in store for me next. My resolve had been sorely tested and my faith in any spiritual beliefs that I might have had are gradually diminishing. However, for the sake of my children, I must be strong and pick myself up and go forward.

I have no doubt that there will be more pain to come in my life but I am prepared to accept it. Only in this way can I be an example to my kids in their life and show them that whatever may be ahead for them in the future you can always get through it.

My life is more settled now and I'm regularly inviting Kevin's friends round to my flat after Sunday sessions in the White Horse for 'choir practice,' in other words a card session until the pub opens again at 7 p.m. Everyone brings round a few cans and on goes the wireless for Top Of The Pops with Alan Freeman in the chair with his famous phrase, *Hi There Pop Pickers,* and then the exodus back to the White Horse for opening time.

One particular incident sticks in my mind. It was during the Christmas period that about eight of Kevin's friends came round for a session after leaving the pub, you could say we were well tanked up and were game for a laugh. I can't really explain why but I was always stocked out with several bottles of Fairy liquid. It was a freezing cold evening and I suggested that we all go down the Old Pond and lather up the fountain. Everyone was game, there was Paul O'Shea, Tony Doolan, Darren Price, Kevin, Ricky West, Gary Vanner, myself and a couple of others whose names I can't remember.

There was a forty foot Christmas tree right in the middle next to the fountain. Within minutes there appeared the biggest bubble bath you've ever seen and we were all splashing about in the pond which must have been well below freezing. The ironic part about it, was that it was all taking place about 100 yards from Cheshunt nick. It wasn't long before the Old Bill were called by a local grass and it sounded like a Second World War air raid as they converged on us from all sides. The more athletic of us did a runner while half a dozen of us got our collar felt, one of which was me, the instigator.

Myself and five others were taken to Enfield nick, soaking wet and freezing cold we were banged up for the night in the cells. I did manage to get a couple of hours kip before I was interrogated and along with the others were allowed to leave and make our own way home as best as we could at about 10 a.m. next morning. It was inevitable that sometime in the coming weeks we would be invited to attend the County Court to explain our presence in the Old Pond fountain.

We were summoned to appear at Hertford County Court and duly obliged. I must say that the Judge was very sympathetic in his summing up and after giving me a dressing down, telling me, as the senior member of the incident, I was responsible and should have known better. We were all then fined £5 and the judge politely asked the prosecution not to waste tax payers money in the future as being Christmas it was all done in high spirits and no harm was done. We all walked away with our tail between our legs and £5 worse off.

It was soon after this that I met another musical personality, Buster Meikle, in my newly adopted local The Green Drago

Buster was a guitarist and member of the group Unit Four Plus Two who had a hit in 1965 with *Concrete and Clay*. He was still working the pubs and clubs as a solo artist and this particular evening he was doing a gig in the Green Dragon. He was still good and drew quite a following. He would always finish his evening with his hit song, which would always bring the punters to their feet in a cynical kind of way. I liked Buster but he did like a drink and although harmless, became the butt of his fellow drinkers jokers who liked to egg him on and take the piss. Unfortunately, he made a rod for his own back by always getting drunk.

There was one occasion when he was booked to play, he was great until the pints started to accumulate on the table in front of him and by 9.30 p.m. he was visibly rockin', not in the accepted sense but the slur had taken over and he was hitting a few bum chords. He was due to take a break and I saw my chance. He knew that I played guitar and did some singing, a bit before his time though and I asked him if I could take over while he was having a break. He agreed and I was playing the great Buster's guitar. After it was announced that Ron would be taking over for the next thirty minutes, a kind of silence followed

I strapped on the guitar. I thought I'd do something a bit different and started to play. *Now this here's the story of the Rock Island Line*, a hit by Lonnie Donegan in 1956. Well, it went down a bomb. There were shouts for more so I dug another Donegan number out, *My Old Man's a Dustman,* by this time I was becoming more confident and followed up with *Puttin on the Style*, which became a No.1 for Lonnie in 1957 and topped the charts for nineteen weeks. It was all over too quickly and I handed the guitar back to Buster with calls of "We want Ron, we want Ron." I thanked Buster and told him I was privileged to have played his guitar which believe me I was. We became great friends after that and one evening he introduced me to Eddie Kidd, the motor bike stunt rider, who had suffered terrible injuries in one of his stunts and was now living in Cheshunt.

Meanwhile in the betting shop where I worked I struck up a working relationship with the local Chinese staff at what was then called Green Dragon Restaurant. It all started when five of them came in the shop and one particular gentleman whose name was Liu came up to me and asked if I fancied anything. Having, at that time, worked for the company for fourteen years I obviously had learned something about the racing game. I had already marked my card and fancied one particularly strongly out of those I had selected. I drew his attention to it and watched as he wrote out the name of this horse, sweating profusely as he put £50 to win on it. The betting show opened for the race in question and I told him not to take the first show but wait to see what happened. Well the horse drifted in the betting from 9/1 to 12/1 so he asked the cashier for 12/1. The horse duly obliged and every Chinese in the shop had backed it. I think between them they won about £2,500.

On the way out they all handed me a bit of paper money in all totalling £125. Unfortunately, this didn't go unseen by the shop manager who pulled me aside and asked me what was occurring. I put him in the frame and he told me that any perks should be shared three ways as there were three staff working in the shop. I thought how come, that don't sound right to me as I'm sussing out the winners. Anyway it was time to have a word with Liu and tell him he had to be more discreet and bung me out of sight of the manager. He understood what I was saying and we worked out an arrangement. All the Chinese lads got the hump with the manager and where in the past they had given him a drink, which incidentally I knew nothing about, he now got nothing when they had a draw. Of course not every horse I tipped was a winner for them but for those in the know one 10/1 winner is equal to ten even money losers providing the stake money is the same.

One afternoon after racing had finished Liu approached and asked me to bring my life to the restaurant and the meal would be on him whatever I wanted be it Chinese or English. I wasn't sure at the time what 'life' meant, did he mean the Sporting Life, the racing paper of the day, no, he meant wife! Well I didn't have a wife so I asked my daughter Dawn if she would like to accompany me to the Green Dragon restaurant as we were being treated to a three course meal courtesy of the staff. Dawn agreed to come with me. Liu pulled me over at one stage and complimented me on my beautiful wife. I said, "Thank you," not letting on. What a wonderful evening!

Liu was a racing fanatic. From experience, the Chinese are the greatest gamblers in the world. Monday came around and Liu came straight up to me and said, "I want to buy a two year old racehorse, will you come to the Newmarket Sales and point out a good horse?" "Hold up," I replied, "I'm not that clever, no, you'll have to do that without me." We didn't pursue the matter further.

The last I heard of him he had gone back to Hong Kong and, believe it or not, had opened up his own Fish and Chip shop. What a character!

# 15

## 1982 - 1991 Jacki

I became acquainted with another young lady who was residing with friends on the top floor of the tower block. I would occasionally see her around the area and we seemed to catch each other's eye and now and then we stopped to have a friendly chat. Little did I know then but these brief encounters were to have a long term and profound effect on my life as you will see as my story unfolds.

The year was 1982 and I am trying to make my bedsit into something resembling a home. The fact that I was a painter and decorator came in useful and it took me about six months to make it look presentable. As my living area was a 9ft x 18ft room, as you can imagine, I wouldn't be able to get much furniture in there. I purchased a three piece suite of which the three seater settee was also a put-u-up bed. By the time that was installed there was no space in the room to put a table so I had to eat my meals with a tray on my lap, but this was no big deal, what the hell, I had a home of my own. There was a small kitchen and a just as small toilet and bathroom.

One evening, it must have been about 10.30 p.m. I was engrossed in a particular programme on my 14 inch TV when my doorbell rang, as I didn't expect anyone I called out "Who is it." It turned out to be the young lady who I mentioned earlier. I immediately opened the door and after speaking to her for a minute or so invited her in as she was very distraught and after making her a cup of tea I asked her what the matter was. She told me that the couple she was living with had told her to leave and that she had nowhere to go. Curious to know what her problem was and maybe help her to resolve it I decided that she could stay in my flat for the night and we would discuss it the next day. In order to allay any fears she might have I made up a bed for her on the floor consisting of three cushion seats off the settee and made up a pillow and a cover, not that it was cold in the flat but just to make her as comfortable as possible. I slept on the put-u-up.

I didn't have to be in to work until 9 a.m. the next morning so being the trusting person that I am I told her she could stay until I came home if she wanted to. Obviously my mind was working overtime during the day and when I came home I found another female friend of hers in the flat. I didn't have a problem with this until I found an empty vodka bottle and two glasses in the kitchen. After asking the other lady to politely leave I asked for an explanation.

That's when we sat down and she told me exactly what was happening in her life. She began by telling me her name, Jacqueline Rogers, she lived with her parents in a bungalow in Enfield near Ordnance Road. Her father was a businessman who did re-decs and renovation work for Haringey Borough Council. He was quite wealthy and also owned a bar in Spain where he paid someone to run it for him. Jacqueline was an only child and her friends knew her as Jacki. My mind was working overtime and I kept asking myself why wouldn't she be at home when her father was so well off.

Jacki seemed keen to tell me that when she was in her early twenties her mother had been diagnosed with a brain haemorrhage, which was terminal. As it turned out her mother was completely reliant on her and in the end Jacki just couldn't cope with the burden of looking after her day in day out while her father was at work. To cut a long story short she decided to leave home and although there were a few gaps along the way, that is what eventually brought her into my life. I was confused and didn't know what to think. However, I gave her the benefit of the doubt and asked if she was still in contact with her family. Jacki said she phoned her father every day to ask how her mother was. Apparently, because he needed to carry out his contractual work he paid a lot of money to keep her in a good nursing home, after Jacki left home. I decided to let her stay in my flat until she could find alternative accommodation. I myself still had doubts about her but could not turn her away as she was homeless.

I have to admit that at one particular time I received an electric bill that I couldn't pay and to my surprise Jacki said she would ask her dad to lend her the money and that she would pay him back. She was as good as her word and after visiting him on the Sunday in question she came back with the money which was £180. This gesture of goodwill meant a lot to me and broke down a trust barrier that I had created myself. Needless to say, I paid every penny back and this impressed her father who then wanted to meet me. I do not know what picture had been painted of me but I knew he would be shocked and surprised to find out that I was twenty years Jacki's senior.

It was arranged that he would come down and pick us up and we would have dinner at his place, a bungalow in Cedars Avenue, just off the Hertford Road in Enfield. I made myself look presentable and at precisely 2 p.m. on the Sunday he turned up in his flash Jag and drove us back to his place.

Her mother had come home for the weekend and I must admit to feeling very out of place. Talking to her mother was hard work as her condition had deteriorated over recent months, but I did my best to converse, that's all I could do. I must say I was very impressed with what I saw. Jacki's father introduced himself to me by saying "Call me Reg." All that I had doubted about what she had told me about her father was dispelled once I was in the bungalow. I was shown around, there was one large room which contained a full sized snooker table and a bar full of every drink you could imagine. Reg made me feel quite at ease but there was still that feeling that we were classes apart. While Jacki spent time with her mother, Reg and I were getting to know a bit about each other. Our first meeting seemed to go down okay although I felt I was being looked down on as not quite up to his family's standard.

During our, what you might call, bonding session I learnt one hell of a lot about his daughter and the family in general. I learned why she gave up her comfortable way of living and left home at age twenty-four years. Jacki had previously told me that as young as she had become the everyday carer of her mother while her father continued to run his business not thinking about the pressure that his daughter was under every day of her young life.

Reg also told me that Jacki had become a drinker and that several times he had confronted her because he had found that newly bought bottles of spirits were vanishing from the bar. Jacki denied all knowledge of this, but her father had found the empty bottles dropped behind a wall at the bottom of the garden. This appeared to be the reason for either Jacki leaving home or on the other hand being asked to leave.

I prefer to side with the former as Reg would have no one to care for his wife and wouldn't be able to carry on his business pursuits. In the first months of our relationship I learned so much about Jacki, the absence of any social life and everything that a person of that age should be doing and the things that she should be learning. To add to her dilemma, she was unfortunate enough to mix or fall in with the wrong people. Jacki named herself as, The Poor Little Rich Girl. I understood where she came from, at that age she was naïve and very vulnerable. Jacki had studied and passed to become a beautician and an expert in make-up. I wanted more than ever to help her and told her she could stay with me indefinitely. I shall never ever regret taking her in but you can make up your own minds whether it was the right thing to do or not. Hindsight is always a great thing but we are not gifted with that quality. I learned to trust her and occasionally would give her money to get shopping and now and then gave her something for herself. Jacki would cook for me and my trust in her grew steadily.

At that time, I was back to doing three jobs. I worked from 6 a.m. to 10 a.m. as a cleaner at the then new Tesco store at Brookfield Lane. When I finished there, I carried on my job as a cleaner at a local pub called The Boozer, which was originally called the Haunch of Venison in Cheshunt High Street. I worked there until 12 noon and then went to my third job which was in a betting shop at the Old Pond. I finished there at about 6 p.m. which for me rounded off a twelve hour stint.

It was round about this time that I decided to get in touch with Ginger, my brother, who was now living in Athens. I got his address from our sister Barbara and wrote and told him what was happening at home and in my life in particular. It turned out that he was doing very well, had formed his own band and was touring Greece and Turkey and making a name for himself. While he was touring and performing in Izmir, Turkey, there was an earthquake which frightened the life out of him, but he soldiered on regardless and finished the concert. I would have liked to have been in touch with him more often but as always, circumstances didn't allow and we contacted each other whenever possible.

The relationship between Jacki and myself had entered a new phase and although there were quite a few doubts in my mind I was prepared to give her the benefit of the doubt and put my trust in her. I so wanted to give her a chance and for her to prove to me that she was worth the effort I was putting in and could help her in some way.

I really liked my cleaning job in the The Boozer and the manager was very impressed with my work. One day while in general conversation with him he mentioned that he wanted to upgrade the pub, redecorate inside and out and have mirrors put up everywhere in the bar to make it look more like a nightclub. This was right up my street as I knew the trade inside out and had done a five year spell at window cleaning which covered the mirror aspect of the job.

All those people who were local to Cheshunt and did a bit of clubbing would know that the manager's previous location was the night-club called Rifles which was in Ordnance Road, off Enfield Highway. The manager's name was Teddy Brown. I never, ever, let him down and to show his appreciation, as I was getting money in the hand, he said that he would legitimise everything and would pay my income tax. The renovation of the premises worked wonders and before too long weekends would bring a full house. He was now catering for a younger clientele and the weekend karaoke went down very well. Teddy would asked me to get the ball rolling by being the first one to go up on stage and do a couple of numbers, this worked a treat. That's another job I had for five years. I was quite a hit with all the young ladies who named me Rockin' Ron. My day finished about 5.30 p.m. in the betting shop and it took me all of twenty minutes to walk home.

Things were not going too well as far as Jacki was concerned. I came in from work most days to find her in bed. This had been going on for a couple of years now and I was virtually her carer. There was the odd occasion that I came home and I was greeted at the door with a hug and a "How's your day been?" I needed to sit down with her and have a heart to heart talk. When I told her this she just said, "Wait until you've had your dinner, I've cooked something special for you." I wasn't going to spoil her moment. Jacki had such a persona about her that I let my guard down and, in spite of her human failing to control her inner-self, I learned that this Jekyll and Hyde character was a wonderful human being who just needed help. I took on the task of giving her the love and affection that had been missing in her life from her parents. I became a father figure, a mentor, a best friend a big brother and a lover.

Our relationship was sweet and sour but I must admit to being deeply disturbed about her physical condition when I eventually found out that she was a confirmed alcoholic. I was going to give her all the love and support that she desperately needed to get out of the dark place she was in. I wanted to believe that I could change her life and make her the happiest person on the planet. As she was now my companion and partner, I would be steadfast in my efforts. I decided to do what her father wouldn't do and that was to trust her by giving her money to buy groceries and if she came through that test successfully, I would reward her with a present for herself to buy anything other than drink. I thought this was working well as she was cooking for me and giving me the change from whatever money I gave her. This wasn't to last and after two or three months I would find personal things missing and half empty bottles of spirit hidden away in cupboards.

I now knew that I was getting into something I knew little about but my feelings for her and her wellbeing overruled any misgivings I had about the problems she was facing at such a young age. Maybe I was out of my depth, but I was going to do everything I could to take her out of the despair she was going through and the downward spiral that I could empathise with and that I had come through over the last few years of my life. I can tell you now, I don't know how I managed to achieve so little when I gave so much. I seemed to be fighting a losing battle and felt time desperately slipping away.

**A setback**

Quite a few things had turned over in my mind now and I felt that I could change her direction and bring her back to the real world without pressure, without torment and without the dreaded alcohol. I really thought my strategy was working until I missed something that had been around for ages, some old 40's and 50's coins that I had been collecting. I decided that, if I wanted my strategy to take effect with Jacki I would bite the bullet and not mention the old coins that had gone missing, although I was strongly tempted. I was now looking for things to disappear but over the next six months I couldn't fault her. Nothing disappeared. I was more confident now than ever that she was turning the corner. I could see by her mannerisms that she was fighting an inner battle but hoping all the time that she was strong enough in body and mind to overcome her demons.

One evening on returning home from work earlier than usual I found she had company, it was the young lady that had been her flatmate on the top floor from where she had been evicted some years previously. I immediately flew into a rage and without asking any questions bodily ejected her from the flat. The reason for losing my temper was an almost one litre bottle of vodka on the table and two glasses both empty.

I needed to calm down and perhaps take a more lenient view. I asked Jacki for an explanation and after turning everything over in my mind thought about what my next course of action would be. At the best of times I am not the most patient of people, but I can be very understanding.

What was it about Jacki that made me feel so sorry for her? Could it be that my feelings for her and my real need to want to help her were blinding me to the reality of her problem. I think that the contributing factor was that when not in drink she was the most generous, loving, person that I'd had the good fortune to meet. I really wanted to understand her reasons at such a young age of twenty years old for turning to the bottle and leaving home when, being an only child, she could have had literally anything she wanted.

During the next six years I learned so much about her from her father that I began to see the reason for her downward spiral through alcohol and near vagrancy. I notified the local council that she was now a permanent resident at my address. Notification was also given to the Enfield authorities and her father that any correspondence relating to her should be addressed to my residence. I do not intend to state further what her reasons were for leaving home but for her they were obviously justified, and it was not my place to judge her one way or the other. I had now made my bed and was going to have to lie on it. I had made a commitment to do all I could to help her and I was determined to carry that out to the bitter end whatever that may be.

As I was devoting so much time to Jacki's wellbeing I needed to have an outlet for my own emotions so took up running the pool team at my local the Green Dragon. We played at home one week and away the next. I remember this week we were playing at the E.W.M.C. the Enfield Working Men's Club at Enfield Highway. They were one of the best teams in the league and after ten games it was five each, with one game to play, being Captain I decided I would contest the last game. It was close but I emerged the winner to the delight of the team and our band of followers. There were no cups or trophies to be won, only pride. I was over the moon and couldn't wait to get home and tell Jacki the news. I must mention that at that time the whole of Grove House was being renovated externally and was surrounded by scaffolding. This particular night I didn't have a key in my pocket as I knew Jacki was staying in. I buzzed the flat but got no answer, tried again and again with no joy, chucked a few stones up at the window, as you do, I started shouting and calling, nothing happened.

Obviously, Jacki had fallen asleep so now I've got problems. I was fucking freezing, it was mid January, so decided on a plan of action. I would scale the scaffolding and climb in through the fanlight window. This was four feet wide and one foot deep. As it happened, I was really skinny then and hit the scales at just nine stone. If I had been the least bit sober no way would I have attempted to do what I did. However, the window overlooked the bed and I slithered through and landed right on top of Jacki who, believe it or not, didn't move a muscle. I decided that I would leave it until the morning to sort things out as I was tired and couldn't be dealing with any domestic upsets at the time which was about 1.30 a.m.

The next day I had words and got so infuriated with her response that in my temper I told her she would have to leave as I didn't want or need all the aggro. Jacki agreed to go later that day and became quite aggressive. The time was getting on now and I think by leaving it late into the evening she thought I might relent. However, I stuck to my guns and she left about 9.30 p.m.

After an hour or so I felt strangely alone and started worrying about where she was and what she was doing. I must admit to feeling guilty as, knowing she had a drinking problem, she could end up anywhere and being a very attractive lady, she would have no trouble attracting undesirable characters.

At about 12.30 a.m as I lay in bed, unable to go to sleep, I heard what I thought was a faint knock on my door. Peeping through my little peephole I saw Jacki outside. Although I was so relieved to see her, I didn't let my true feelings out of the bag. I let her in and made her a cuppa and she burst out crying. I couldn't help but comfort her and we sat up till the early hours having a meaningful conversation about the path that we should go down if she wanted to stay with me. There had to be some rule changes, if that was possible, although I didn't really know the task ahead.

Because I'm human and knowing she was such a warm and caring person, away from alcohol, I was prepared to accept responsibility for her as long as she was prepared to seek help whatever the final outcome. It was now down to her to prove that she was serious about this. Her visits to the Royal Free Hospital in Hampstead became less and I could see a willingness that for six years I hadn't seen before. I was coming home from work in the evening and was being greeted by a different person. She was making herself up and looking beautiful for me and also cooking special meals every evening. Where I used to come home from work every evening and find her in bed intoxicated, I was receiving a welcome fit for a king. This went on for several months, she was still on a lot of medication which was so important to her at this stage in her recovery programme. Jacki's father had now accepted me with open arms and was over the moon, not only with the progress his daughter was making but his very welcome acceptance of my help in getting her back on track in the real world. My efforts were so appreciated by him that he couldn't do enough for me.

To give just one example he told me to go to Cheshunt Council and ask the price needed to buy the flat outright on leasehold which was for 100 years. The actual value of the property was £54,000. But because I had been a resident of Cheshunt for twenty-eight years the asking price was £18,000 which was exactly one third of the valuation. On telling him this we were invited to dinner at his bungalow on the coming Sunday. He laid out his plan to Jacki and I and short of signing on the dotted line plans were arranged for himself and his solicitors to visit the flat and lay out the details. With all the concerned parties present his solicitor read out the details of the plan. Mr Rogers i.e. Jacki's father would hand over a cheque for £18,000 and buy the property.

There were conditions however which his solicitor briefed us on and which we decided to accept. The property would be split three ways. Myself, Jacki and her father. All three of us signed the legal documents to this effect along with the solicitor involved. Of course it all had to be legalised by Broxbourne Council before our plans could be finalised. The purchase was accepted and in 1989 the property officially became ours. There were two main stipulations that Reg put down. Firstly, I would be responsible for paying the maintenance bills and service charges and any other monies that had to be paid concerning the flat. The second was more of a gentlemen's agreement than a stipulation. Each one of us would sign to become triple joint owners, at that time this was

Jacki, Reg and myself. In the event of any of the parties pre-deceasing the others the property would then be owned by the other two. Then whoever pre-deceased the other joint owner would become the sole owner of the property. I thanked Reg and his reply was thank you for all you've done for my daughter. This was Reg's way of thanking me for looking after his daughter for the previous seven years.

I got to see more of Reg over that year and we were invited to several functions that he attended with other businessmen. One event was an amateur boxing tournament at the Starlight Rooms in Southbury Road, Enfield. That was followed by an auction of Spurs memorabilia, on which he spent a few quid. He noticed the difference in Jacki's behaviour too and how she was only drinking soft drinks instead of alcohol. In a way I sympathised with him as his wife was in a private hospital being treated for a brain disorder and his only daughter was a confirmed alcoholic. How sad is that?

**The Proposal**

It was September 1990 now and I arranged, on the 10th of the month which was my 54th birthday, to take Jacki out for a meal. She must have spent the day making herself look beautiful. I finished work early in order to prepare for our special occasion. I had a big surprise for her which was about to rock our world.

After we'd finished our meal I plucked up courage and proposed to her. The look on her face was something to behold and, after a few seconds, she burst into tears and said I thought you'd never ask me. I can't tell you how emotional the moment was. We decided to wait until our next visit to her dad for dinner which was the following Sunday to break the news. As regular as clockwork Reg turned up in his flash Jaguar XJ6, went through all the usual greetings and bollocks and we all drove off not knowing what his reaction was going to be.

*Me and Jacki*

While Reg's voice was rambling on and on about his work I was trying to figure out how I was going to break the news about Jacki and our engagement. I decided that after we'd sat down for a while, after dinner, I'm going in. I keep looking over at Jacki and she is saying softly, "now, now." Finally, I pluck up courage and offered him a game of snooker. I then said, "Reg, I have something to tell you." I was trying to be as diplomatic as possible but that wasn't working so, as he was about to pot the blue ball I just came out with it. "Reg, Jacki and I have decided we want to get married." When he said, "Oh have you now." my heart sank and I was lost for words. This is déjà vu, I've been here before. He then called his daughter into the snooker room and asked her if it was true. Jacki nervously replied, "Yes, Dad it is." His next words were, "I think we should let your mother know." Jacki replied, "I've already told her." Reg then said, "For what Ron has done for you and what he has achieved in the last eight years I give you both my blessing."

With relief and lots of emotion I had come through the second most emotional chapter of my life. Reg started making arrangements there and then and no one else could get a word in. He said he would pay for everything and not to worry about a thing. I need to add that as her mother was suffering from a tumour on the brain she wasn't quite aware of what was going on. Although, I knew of Jacki's efforts to get herself clean of drink I knew I had a mammoth task still in front of me but was prepared more than ever to try and put her back together again. This was now my sole purpose in life and I truly wanted to succeed.

In the days and weeks ahead all we did was discuss plans for the wedding. Jacki's excitement and enthusiasm was a sight to behold. I told her to slow down and let's take one step at a time. Firstly, we must arrange the date of the big day and then discuss and plan all the details. We agreed to set the date for 15th June 1991. Jacki was a very good organiser so, unless she asked me, I let her have the reins. The initial exuberance died down somewhat as her father wanted to get in on the act and rightly so as he was financing the big day.

## Light at the end of the tunnel

After eight long years there seemed to be a light at the end of the tunnel. It was now Christmas 1990 and I had the biggest surprise of my life when Jacki, for the first time in eight years, had stopped drinking and was now under the Royal Free Hospital as a recovering alcoholic. I couldn't count the number of pills that she had to take daily.

This was a far cry from when she had to appear at Highbury Magistrates Court for fraud when collecting benefit from two different departments, Islington and Enfield. Jacki was terrified what the outcome of this would be and thought she may have to go to prison. I told her not to worry and that I would go to court with her and support her. Unbeknown to her I wrote a letter and got the court usher to hand it to the judge. After summing up the judge read the letter out in court and asked to see us both after the trial. He then told Jacki that it was because of the letter I'd written that he had decided to give her another chance to change her life but she would have to pay back the money that she received under false pretences. She was also committed to do Community Service for three months which she did supervising children in the V and E youth centre in Goffs Lane which she liked.

After seeing out 1990 there were lots of things to discuss and lots of plans to be made. With a little over six months to the big day there was so much to organise.

I was still working two jobs and actually took on a third job as a cleaner at the big Tesco store at Brookfield Lane. Within two weeks I was made supervisor cleaner when the existing one left the company. Then the opening time was 9 a.m. but I had to be there by 5 a.m. As well as supervising I took on the job as window cleaner too. There I go again doing three jobs daily, roughly twelve hours a day but at least we had the evening and night-time to ourselves. Jacki and her father were in constant communication planning for our special day. January 1991 disappeared without trace and the excitement and intensity grew as February slipped by. We had both notified our nearest and dearest about plans for the wedding but not the details as yet. March 2nd 1991 was a Saturday and as always a very busy racing day. Every moment spent at home now with Jacki was real quality time for us both. I was 99% sure now that she'd won her battle with her demons, in fact I was confident.

**Was it ever meant to be?**

Regularly, while working on Saturday, Jacki would give me a quick phone call, much to the chagrin of the manager who was a bit of a jobsworth and didn't like me using the company phone for personal calls. It was only a couple of minutes so I just ignored his comments. This particular day for some reason she didn't ring. I carried on with my daily routine not worrying too much as I knew she would be waiting for me outside the shop when I left.

When I'd finished and left my work she wasn't there to meet me, I must admit to being a bit concerned. It would normally take me about twenty minutes to walk home over the A10, across the New River and up through the park. Today was different, it took me roughly twelve minutes. As usual, Scotty, our little terrier, was barking with excitement as I neared the door of the flat. I decided to knock and wait for Jacki to open the door. After a minute or so I fumbled for my key and let myself in as she hadn't opened the door. I found her lying in bed absolutely oblivious. I can't tell you the thoughts that raced through my mind. I tried to wake her by calling her name but got no response. I shook her arm several times but again I failed to wake her. I immediately took hold of her arm and with bated breath felt for a pulse. What I felt at this time was complete panic and dismay. I grabbed the phone and spoke to her doctor telling him I had an emergency. I was told to ring the emergency service and get her an ambulance. Apparently the doctor was in his surgery and had a room full of patients. After waiting 40 minutes and still no ambulance I lost control and ran to the doctor's surgery which was three minutes away in Cromwell Avenue. I had already knocked up my next door neighbour and asked him to listen for the paramedics and left him the key to my front door. I will relate later what went off at the doctors.

When I got back to the flat the ambulance had arrived. On telling them the situation I was asked quite a few questions, telling them she was a recovering alcoholic and to my knowledge had not had a drink for about seven months. On wandering round to the far side of the bed one of them found a blue plastic washing up bowl that was half full of black liquid. On closer examination he said he needed to get her to hospital as soon as possible and that it was a serious emergency. One of them brought in a wheelchair and we all lifted her into it.

I was stunned and felt very sick. I threw several things together for her and gave them a purse with some money in for her. Before pulling away one of the paramedics said that she had regained consciousness but was in pain. With that they left me standing in the parking area of Grove House.

A feeling of desolation swept over me as I returned to my flat to be greeted by Scotty. I sat and waited for Jacki to call, it seemed like hours. I wanted to ring the hospital but decided I was over reacting. It was 8.35 p.m. when my phone rang, my heart was pumping so fast, I couldn't answer it. It went over to answer phone: message for Ronald Hepting to please ring reception at Chase Farm Hospital and that it was a matter of urgency. A number was given and I suddenly felt very sick.

I finally plucked up courage to contact them and was put in contact with a senior doctor. After confirming who I was I was given the devastating news that Jacki had passed away having received seven pints of blood in transfusions. I actually felt the emotion in the doctor's voice. I was in complete shock but it was to hit me a lot harder when the realisation dawned a couple of hours later. After collecting my thoughts I rang my daughter who lived in Waltham Cross. Dawn and her husband were at my flat within fifteen minutes. Dawn said to get some things together and come to stay with them for a while. I told her I couldn't go without taking Scott the dog and Charlie the budgie. At this time, I said I needed to contact Jacki's father. Kim, Dawn's husband, said we would do that just as soon as we got to their place.

We couldn't contact Jacki's father anywhere, being a Saturday night he was most probably out at some business dinner with colleagues or at his local snooker club or maybe the Starlight Rooms and club in Southbury Road, Enfield. Eventually a message was left for him to ring Dawn's number when he arrived home.

It was about midnight when the house phone rang, Kim answered it and it was Reg asking to speak to me. Telling Jacki's father what had happened that night was one of the hardest things I've ever had to do in my life. I will not dwell on his reaction. I informed him also that I was staying at my daughter's and that he could contact me there. I needed to clear my mind before I could make any plans to meet Reg and tell him everything and to make any arrangements that needed to be made.

After a couple of days I built up my mental strength to visit Reg at his bungalow to obtain the necessary documents, visit the coroner's offices in Enfield and to start making arrangements for Jacki's funeral. Reg wanted to have a heart to heart talk with me and he took me to a restaurant for dinner. Suffice to say I had no appetite and left most of what was on my plate.

One thing about that night was nagging at me constantly and it was important to me that I got the answer to my question. The coroner's report stipulated that the cause of death was cirrhosis of the liver and on Saturday 2nd Mar 1991 Jacki's liver ceased to function. All other organs were classified as 'unremarkable' which meant they were all functioning normally. My question was that as Jacki had died as a result of liver failure, due to her alcohol addiction, was there any trace of alcohol in her system whatsoever when she passed away? I must say here and now that there was no trace of alcoholic substance found in her body and that the alcoholic abuse she had inflicted upon herself over the past twenty years of her very young life had finally taken its toll. I trusted her implicitly and she repaid my trust in her absolutely. Jacki died aged just thirty-four years. In the aftermath of all that had happened I built up a very strong and close relationship with her father.

This was a very hard time for me and I became somewhat of a hermit. Come the day of the funeral my flat became the leaving place for her family and friends the majority of whom I would never see again. I was given the freedom of Grove House car park for three hours on the morning of March 16th 1991. I couldn't wait to get the day over and mourn in my own way and to do this I needed to be alone.

The next day I brought all the flowers back and shared them between all the elderly people in the sheltered wing of Grove House.

Six months after the tragic events of March 1991 I had built up my case and felt strong enough to take the doctor to court having refused to visit Jacki on what I can now call her deathbed.

Reg came with me and congratulated me on my resolve to go through with this. I won't go into the details of what happened in this case but just to say this. For an individual to take a member of the Medical Council to court is a complete waste of time. It was no more than a kangaroo court which I had lost before it started. Try breaking in to Fort Knox!!!. In some ways I had some semblance of satisfaction. Six months later the same doctor had a care home above his surgery in Cromwell Avenue closed down because of neglect of his elderly patients. Crumbs of comfort but never, never any compensation.

For the sake of my family I really needed to get my life back on track again and somehow find light again as I was constantly in a very dark place. My first priority was my job and having taken three weeks off I, for more than one reason, needed to get back and carry on doing the two jobs I was happy doing. It was so strange but it seemed to me that associates and friends seemed to be avoiding me. I guess destiny has taken me down a few different roads in my life and I had no idea of where the next turning would be.

I kept in regular contact with Reg up until the day his wife passed on which, incidentally, was just six months later. How cruel to lose your daughter and your wife in the space of just six months. It left a mark on his health and he confided in me that the climate in the UK was not good for him and that he planned to move abroad, Tenerife in fact.

We did lose regular contact after he moved but we both sent Christmas cards to one another each year. It was during this time that he told me that in future I would be wholly responsible for paying the maintenance or service charges on my flat. Roughly it worked out to about £1,000 annually but varied yearly depending what money was spent on the block during the previous year. I carried on my life as usual at work but lost touch with the outside world.

# 16

## Fight For Life


In 1993 two years after Jacki's passing I noticed that my voice was becoming very husky and occasionally it disappeared completely. As it always seemed normal the next day I put it to the back of my mind and assumed it was just a virus of some sort. After three months it hadn't worsened but had not got any better. My first instinct was my vocal chords and did I have what singers call nodules.

A friend of mine Stevie Phelps was resident musician in a local pub called The Rising Sun in Hammond Street Road, Nobby Dalton of ex Kinks fame was also a group member there. I decided to test my voice and see if it was normal. I mentioned my problem to Stevie and he asked me if I'd like to sing a number and check it out. He said that if the worst happened and you lose your voice someone will take over on vocals. To cut a long story short the worst did happen and I couldn't finish the song. I apologised to Stevie and hurriedly left the premises. By this time I now knew this had to be checked out.

A couple of days later I took myself to Chase Farm Hospital the last place I wanted to be as that's where Jacki had died. After two hours I was called in and briefly had my throat looked at. I was informed that it looked quite red even though it wasn't sore. I was told to wait and I would be called. Mercifully I only waited twenty minutes before I had a more thorough examination by a throat specialist named, Dr Farag. He performed what's known as an endoscopy. Briefly, both nostrils are sprayed with an anaesthetic which renders them numb, then a tube with a minute camera on the end is inserted into the nose and enters the throat, taking pictures of whatever is there. During this whole process I was gagging like mad until I was told how to relax which was easier to say than to do. After what seemed like an eternity the camera was withdrawn and the diagnosis was drawn. I was told I needed further tests to clarify exactly what the problem was. After those tests I went home and waited for a letter to tell me the news, good or bad.

If you've ever waited for test results by post you will know just how harrowing that wait can be. Finally, after about ten days, my letter came. I was told to make an appointment in the oncology unit for briefing and test results. While waiting in a full waiting room, eventually I was called, I think I shit myself while waiting.

Fortunately, my daughter Dawn accompanied me and was allowed to join me for the result. My worst nightmare was realised when I got the result. I had a cancerous growth on my voice box and would have to undergo rigorous radiotherapy for six weeks. I was to attend the North Middx Hospital and I would be under a certain Dr Karp who would organise my treatment programme. At the time I was informed that the cancer had been diagnosed early which gave me a better chance of beating it. I must add that from that fateful day I never smoked another cigarette. Previously I was getting through a half ounce of Old Holborn a day.

On the way home Dawn, who drove me to the hospital, quite understandably, started to cry. I may have joined her in a few tears but told her to make for the Green Dragon and we'd have a stiff drink or two. On reflection, I think I had a couple of large brandies and we talked at length about arrangements for getting to the hospital for my treatment. Dawn would pick me up every day and wait for me to come home again.

I had to have a papier mache mask made which would cover

my face only exposing the part that would be treated. I was counselled by my radiotherapist before treatment commenced and he said I would not feel a thing until about four weeks into my treatment when I would suffer radiation burns. These were so very painful and unsightly. The advice was to buy a silk scarf for a dual purpose: to cover the burn marks and somewhat ease the pain. It was dreadful.

My throat felt like I was continually swallowing broken glass and I also lost my voice. I was determined to stay positive throughout my ordeal and I feel this was a contributing factor to the positive results of my treatment a month or so later. My first check-up showed that the tumour had gone but that I would have to undergo check-ups for the next year. Wonderful. I couldn't wait to get my voice back for more reasons than one.

The funny side of it all was that I spent most of my time writing notes in the pub until my voice returned. Derek Welsh, a good friend of mine at the time, would mouth words and sentences to me until I said Del-boy I'm not fucking deaf you can talk and I can hear. Obviously I wrote this down…very amusing. Things seemed to progress normally after this episode in my life and normality is a word I don't use lightly.

# 17

## A night to remember

I still had a friend with me, Scotty, my dog who was my constant companion and of course Charlie, the Spurs supporter budgie. It was the dawn of the technological age and within five years it would cost me my job as a boardman in the betting shop industry. Yes, machines were taking over and I, like thousands of others, were being replaced by computers and television monitors. My employers decided to transfer me to one of their shops in Enfield which would add two hours to my day every day six days a week. This also added twelve hours to my working week but nothing extra to my salary.

A petition was signed by more than 400 local punters and regulars in the shop to keep me where I was, this had no effect on the management and within a week I was transferred.

In my local pub, the Green Dragon, I became known as 'Ron The Dog' as you would never see me without Scot. I remember one time there was a local dog show advertised and I entered my dog for the obstacle race. This is where you run him round little obstacles on his lead and he negotiates the obstacles and is awarded points. The amusing part about it was that I negotiated every obstacle while he ran alongside me, the spectators thought it was hilarious and actually gave us a big red rosette for entertainment.

It was now 1996 and Jacki had been gone for five years, my candle burns brightly every March 2nd in memory of our time together before she sadly left me. I got a text from my brother

Monty that Ginger was in England, here from Rhodes, on a break and he was doing a gig in the Lordship pub in Lordship Lane, Tottenham. I got a friend of mine to take me without letting on I was coming. I managed to arrive before he set up but joined Monty and some friends and relations that were with him. Before he was announced I shot out to the loo and came back in when he was all set up. Well, the look on his face when I walked in was of astonishment and then emotion as we hugged each other and yes there were a few tears of joy.

During his interval break we had so much to talk about before he went back on stage. I did make him promise to come to my local, the Green Dragon, next time he was in England. I mentioned it to Keith the manager of the pub, who incidentally knew all about my brother as I never stopped talking about him. He said, next time he's in the country bring him in and we can have a chat.

That's exactly what happened when he next came to England and they both discussed business and arranged for Ginger to do a gig there. It was easy to arrange a date as he was touring the country at that time on a two month break.

Came the day and there was a buzz of excitement in the pub as I had built my brother up to all my friends who were now expecting great things. Ginger arrived with Monty and after a word with the manager was shown where to set up, as there was no stage, but was allotted a quarter of the saloon area to arrange all his kit. At 8.55 p.m. he was announced by Keith as Ron's brother from Rhodes. A ripple of applause ensued and then he went straight into his first number. The song was *Sweet Caroline* by Neil Diamond. Wow!!!, shut your eyes, it was Neil Diamond. A rapturous applause with shouts of more, more and only after one song he had won everybody over. To be honest, I think he was very surprised. I think a lot of people were apprehensive at first but very soon came to appreciate the talents of a very fine musician and all round guitarist and vocalist. The first hour passed too quickly for the audience but a break for him was very welcome. The crowd was absolutely buzzing when he opened his second session.

Ginger invited people up to sing, a karaoke, more or less. A space was made for dancing and by 10.30 p.m. the place was really rocking. Then came request time. I was so overwhelmed, had he really come this far? He was amazing and I was so proud of him. Incidentally, the pub made a fortune that night and it was no surprise when Keith invited him back to a repeat performance. My brother held out for more than he was offered for another gig and eventually he got what he wanted.

On his previous visit he also asked the manager if he could safely leave some of his equipment in his charge to which he replied, yes OK. A very valuable amplifier was left. From time to time I would ask the manager where it was stored and he told me in a big shed lock up near the rear of the pub. On one particular occasion I walked in the Dragon and to my surprise I noticed the amplifier in the Saloon Bar underneath one of the long bench seats. I was assured it would be safe there as there was only three days to go before Ginger was due to play. Incidentally the bar was being re-carpeted and would be finished on the Friday the day before the gig. I didn't give it another thought. I wasn't told until the Saturday evening, arriving earlier than normal, that the amplifier had disappeared. I didn't even have time to inform Ginger that he didn't have an amplifier. On arrival, when told, he was shocked and annoyed but as they say in show business the show must go on.

Fortunately there were lots of friends in the pub and one particular friend Brian Kew worked in another local pub called, The Jolly Bricklayers. My son eventually got him to drive back to that pub and borrow an amplifier for the evening. To say the evening went well would be an understatement. It was a fabulous night and also a very emotional one for Ginger and I. It was suggested by a family friend that I get up and do a song. My confidence hadn't gone but would my voice stand up to it after all the treatment and trauma of my cancer recovery. I couldn't turn the opportunity down nor the chance to sing with my brother. Ironically, I chose to sing *Whole Lotta Shakin'*, the same song I did when I last sang in public two years earlier. I managed to get through it without a hitch and at the end we hugged, both wallowing in tears of overwhelming joy and profound emotion.

After Monty and Ginger left that night I found a new friend who admired my brother Ginger's musical talent, becoming a great friend and admirer of what he stood for and what he was achieving in the tourist business of the Greek island of Rhodes. I made a promise that night that at my earliest convenience I would take a holiday on the island to get together for a reunion and try to relive some of the happiest moments we'd spent during our young musical careers.

# 18

## Return to Braunston

Not long after this in July of the year 2000 I had a yearning to go back in time and visit the village and people I grew up with in those early years during the war. I contacted Rutland County Council for information. They referred me to Oakham district office as this was the county town of Rutland. They were very helpful and when I told them my reasons they furnished me with information that led to me meeting up eventually with my very old friends.

On the 15th June I set a date for the visit and arranged for my daughter Dawn and son in law Kim to take me. Ironically enough they lived en-route to the destination as their residence is in Mildenhall, Suffolk. Anyway they picked me up in Cheshunt and it took in all about one and three-quarter hours for the journey. It was just as though time had stood still. Nothing looked different and was just how I remembered it. My first task was to find where Isabel lived, she was the lovely, dark haired, daughter of the couple who took me in. We found her address and knocked on her door.

She had no idea who was standing before her so I asked her, "so you don't recognise me?" Her immediate reply was, "No, but with that accent, it can only be one person, Ronald Hepting, the young man who lived with us during the war." We hugged and she welcomed us in to a rather dark, musty and dingy looking living room. I have to say she was now eighty years old. Her long flowing hair was still to her shoulders but a beautiful silver. There were a few tears shed before we got talking about distant memories never forgotten. It was to be expected when she told me her father John and mother Mary had passed some years ago. I don't really know what thoughts were going on in my mind but the first thing I asked her was to take a walk just down the road as I wanted to revisit the farm where we all lived together.

I was devastated when I got there and all I saw were the remnants spread around the field of the home where I grew up as a three year old. There were fragments of a bygone 1930's, milk churns, milking machines, parts of old Fordson tractors and stone building blocks all over the place. My next visit, again at my own request, was the beautiful old Manor House where, as kids, my sister Sylvie and I sat with our name tags round our necks and our evacuee numbers along with gas masks waiting to be chosen and not knowing how it would turn out.

After leaving the farm and the Manor House I decided it was time for a spot of lunch and I knew the only two pubs in the village as they were there from my childhood. It took us five minutes to walk to the Plough where we had a home-made steak and kidney pie with all the trimmings and I washed it down with a couple of pints of local ale while Dawn had a vodka and tonic.

We had pre-arranged to meet with all the friends that I knew as kids back in 1940. Knocking on the door of the contact I had been given I was received with rapturous applause and handshakes all round. I must admit to not recognising any of the gentlemen present at first and then, as I was introduced to each and every one, their names came flooding back to me and it was a reunion that brought laughter and tears even to Dawn.

One person in particular who I did remember was my best friend Dennis Meadows. We were inseparable back then and that bond will stay with me for the rest of my life. I'm looking forward to the summer months when Kevin and his partner Sally will be taking me to visit my old comrades again, for most it may be the last time. Obviously, things may have change by the time I go and some of those dear friends may already have passed on. I know that several months after my first visit dear Isabel passed away. The people who took me in and kept me safe and that I made friends of and the memories that were made, will stay with me forever.

# 19

## Holidays in Rhodes

In 2005 I had saved enough for a two week holiday on the island of Rhodes. I phoned and asked if Ginger could find some accommodation for two at a reasonable price. Fortunately, I had met a lady friend who was willing to accompany me on the trip as I didn't feel I could travel alone.

I was now sixty-nine years old and in all honesty I had never travelled abroad so needed my friend to show me the ropes, so to speak. On the departure day I was so pleased to have this friend with me as they were acquainted with the routine and I was completely lost. We departed from Stansted airport and I had a few gin and tonics in the bar before we finally boarded the plane. We arrived four hours later at Rhodes Airport and even though it was 9 p.m. the warm air embraced us as we came out into the open air.

We waited about ten minutes before I spotted my brother who had arranged to pick us up at the airport. As you can imagine, our initial greetings were intense before making our way to his waiting car.

We were driven to a place called, Angela's Apartments, in a small locality called, Kremasti. After introductions to this wonderful and friendly Greek lady we eventually got to our apartment and I just couldn't wait to get my head down. My friend was in the next apartment to mine and no doubt followed suit after getting into bed. I woke up to the sound of my phone and it was my brother asking if everything was OK.

After exchanging mid-morning greetings I arranged to meet

him later to plan the action for the day. Outside the apartments were a couple of bench seats under a shaded area where we planned to meet each day and exchange views and discuss the day's agenda.

My friend and I decided on our first morning to have a look around and acquaint ourselves with this picturesque little village. My first thoughts were to seek out the local watering hole and to use sign language if I had to. It wasn't long before I struck gold. About 200 yards up the road we found a place called Tommy's Bar and I couldn't believe it when I found out they sold John Smiths bitter, kin ell; home from home. When the staff and punters got to know who I was I was treated like a king as Ginger seemed to be a great friend of everyone on the island. As my brother had his everyday routine to follow, my friend and I decided to discover what we could about the island and which places to go and enjoy ourselves.

It was a twenty minute walk to the beach from our apartment so that's where we started to make our voyage of discovery. It was a beautiful place all lined with deck chairs and sunbeds as far as the eye could see. We chose a spot and settled down to some sunbathing. My friend found interest in reading books. The incoming planes, as they came into Rhodes airport only a couple of miles away, would fly very low over the beach, so not so quiet but great for plane spotting! There was a food and refreshment bar at the back of the beach but we soon learned that the toilet facility was a hole in the ground so we decided to take precautionary measures before leaving the apartment. A very friendly and chatty gentleman came round collecting payment for the sunbeds but when he found out that I was Ken's brother he refused to take my money. As far as I can remember his name was Tassos and he was an ardent admirer of my brother and his music.

In the far distance across the Aegean sea a coastline vaguely appeared through the distant haze which I later learned was the coastline of Turkey. We spent five or six hours on the beach at Kremasti before walking back and preparing for an evening of discovery in the fortifications surrounding the old town of Rhodes, known locally as Rhodos. Going through the main entrance was like hitting a bazaar with lots of stalls selling multi coloured clothes of all descriptions and also very modern shops selling mementos and jewellery and almost everything you may be looking for. It was very quaint and modern at the same time. We kept walking and it wasn't long before the packed streets really narrowed and we found we were being pursued and overtaken by donkeys. Their owners selling donkey rides.

We decided to duck into a small café we came across to have something to eat. I really fancied a cheese and pickle sandwich so with trepidation, and a laugh from my friend, that's what I ordered. I was astounded when I was brought the best cheese and pickle sandwich I've ever tasted. We decided to venture out into the old town again and spent the rest of the time buying nick-nacks and dodging donkeys. After several hours we decided to make our way back to Tommy's Bar and have a couple of John Smiths, my friend had wine. Outside, on the front, there was a pool table so we had a few games to pass the time. After an hour or so we decided to make our way back to the apartment and plan our evening.

I suggested to my friend that we get suitably dressed and go for a meal and then on to the restaurant bar where my brother was playing. We found a Chinese restaurant with an outside eating area and sat in the cool evening breeze. It was most enjoyable. After the meal I called for a cab to take us to The Pegasus bar where Ginger was the resident musician.

At the Pegasus we met the host and compere who was also the manager. I introduced us both and the reception I got from him was truly amazing. He in turn introduced me to his wife and all the staff working on the premises. He just couldn't do enough for us and we were treated like royalty. He went on to tell me that he had the best musician on the island would be starting at 9 p.m. I had already informed Ginger that I would be coming down to the Pegasus for the evening. At roughly 8.15 p.m. he came in with a couple who I got to know as Sissy and Klaus. Ginger ordered a massive dinner of sausages, chips, egg and beans and ate the lot before going on stage. By 9 p.m. the place was full with tourists and locals. I spent most of the evening on the dance floor with my friend as I could still cut a nifty rug, well I was in my prime at sixty-nine years old!

Eventually we called a cab and left the club about 11 p.m. In the few hours that we spent there we made quite a few friends. The following day I phoned Ginger and asked if he would be busy during the day. He told me he had the day to himself so I asked him if he would take me and my friend to Lindos. He said he would and it was about a fifty minute drive. When we arrived he dropped us off and said he would pick us up when we were ready to come back. If ever you visit Rhodes put Lindos in your diary, the scenery is absolutely amazing. We had the most wonderful holiday on the island but as the saying goes all good things come to an end. I must say also that the Greek people are the most welcoming people I have had the privilege to meet. We had a wonderful ten days and were looking forward to the time we could return there. I had to wait another three years until 2008 before I could visit Rhodes and Ginger again.

**Return to Rhodes**

Nothing much changed in my everyday life over the next few years and I settled back into my every day routine of waking, working, eating, drinking and sleeping. Uppermost in my mind was the day I could go back to Rhodes and enjoy the hospitality of the local people and spend some time with Ginger again.

It seemed like a lifetime of waiting but eventually 2008 came round and the friend who accompanied me on the last holiday said they would love to go back again. I was happy to have her along as I don't think I could have booked the holiday without her help. If my memory serves me right we departed Stansted Airport on the 4th September. We arrived four hours later and my brother was waiting for us at the airport. This time we chose an all inclusive holiday in Kalathea.

We acquainted ourselves with the hotel site and were shown to our apartments by very friendly staff. As we were next door to each other we communicated by calling out from the balcony. The seafront was about a twenty minute walk from the apartment and we found a local corner pub which we adopted as our regular and became quite well known in there. I had to fight off vendors trying to sell cheap watches, who incidentally were very vociferous, attitude wise, but they never became a real problem.

On our third day I phoned my brother and asked him when he was free would he take us out for the evening to a place of his choice. He agreed but didn't tell us where we were going. We got to this venue and it was like Soho on a Saturday night!

It turned out to be Faliraki, wow, no one was dressed up and the young kids were in their element. How I yearned for my youth again. I don't remember the name of the taverna but we had a wonderful night out. A meal and a good drink, the ouzo went down like a bomb and so did I when I got back to the hotel. A lot of our evenings were spent at the Pegasus bar and restaurant during our stay and it was a most enjoyable experience.

Alas, it was the penultimate day of the holiday and that day was mostly taken up arranging our departure from the island. The evening had already been arranged for a farewell drink and get together with Ginger at the Pegasus. We got a cab about 7 p.m. and had a meal on arrival also securing our table for the evening. He came in about 8 p.m. and immediately ordered what I would call a massive English breakfast or an almighty fry up. I was sure he wouldn't eat it but he had no problem whatsoever.

Of course, we had a lengthy chat and I noticed that every time he inhaled his chest just rattled. Never being someone who's lost for words I had to mention it to him. Knowing that he was a heavy smoker I asked how his voice stood up to singing and he said it doesn't affect him. I dropped the subject as he was due to start playing. Before he started I said how about me and you doing a duet later, he said I was going to ask you anyway. After having his mid evening break he called me to the stage and we literally said together, *Let It Be Me*, a song we used to sing back in the 60's. I was surprised by the audience's reaction, it went down so well and made me feel like a young twenty-four year old again. It was a bitter sweet occasion as flying home the next day, on 18th September 2008, I didn't even know if I would be fortunate enough to visit the island again.

# 20

## My dear brother and closest friend, Ginger

The time passed so quickly and soon enough it was Christmas. I had been invited by my friend to spend it at their home, which I was very grateful for. I couldn't have been more relaxed and got up Boxing Day about 8.30 a.m. While I was in the kitchen helping with all the clearing up and general chores that needed doing I was told there was a phone call for me. Surprised but not with trepidation I thought it was one of my own family. It was my brother Monty.

I was pretty chirpy and wished him a Merry Christmas and in the next breath he told me that Ginger had died. I was stunned to silence and shocked in the extreme. I remember swearing down the phone to Monty and saying for fuck sake. He was too upset to speak and I had to wait twenty-four hours before I knew what had happened. It brought home to me my very last words to him when he drove us to the airport, "Please go to the hospital and get that chest sorted out." It was at that moment I realised, that if I hadn't told him to get himself checked out he would still be alive today. I withdrew totally into myself over the next three months mourning the passing of my dear brother and my closest friend.

### Tribute to Ginger

On re-emerging to the living world I wanted to pay my final tribute to Ginger by having a memorial plaque made and sent to his resting place in the quiet and pretty cemetery in the small village of Maritsa on Rhodes. I had it made here and then through the company, had it shipped out to the island. After a couple of weeks I sought confirmation with the company as to its arrival in Rhodes. I was horrified and pissed off when I was notified that it had been returned to the UK. A minute spelling error of its destination address caused it to be sent back. On checking again with the company it seems that they had mis-spelt the village name Maritsa and instead sent it to Marista. Why on earth did the receiving company in Rhodes not put two and two together and work it out, after all it's not rocket science.

Within the next four weeks the company admitted liability and paid me £100 in compensation and also paid to have it sent to the correct address. This took another three weeks before it was finally laid in its rightful place. I would also like to thank the people and patrons who bought and placed the beautiful bench next to his grave who all came from Tommy's Bar and also my thanks go to anyone else who donated toward this. Thank you all sincerely. I've haven't managed to go back to Rhodes after this visit so never got to see the memorial plaque that was laid on his stone.

I'm really glad to say that I managed to get in touch with Ginger's beautiful ex-wife Roula, sometime later, and who now lives with her mother in Athens. My dearest wish was to visit Roula, if at all it became possible to do so, but as I get older that wish and desire is diminishing as my body just won't let me do the things I want most of all to do. I try to stay as active as I can and love nothing more than going down the pub as often as is possible and having a small bet. I'm no mug punter by the way and after working in the betting shop for twenty years have some idea of what I'm looking for.

# 21

## A reunion in Tenerife

My next trip abroad was in 2012 to Tenerife. A ten day holiday which I had with my travelling friend. The secondary purpose for making that trip was once more to see Jacki's, my deceased fiancée's, father who moved there in 1994, three years after the death of his only child. It turned out to be a very moving and emotional reunion. He had a trusted lady friend with him and I arranged to take them for dinner the following day where we caught up with all the news in each others lives since the day he moved abroad. Sometime later, I tried several times to contact him on the number that he gave me but somehow or for some reason or another I lost touch as his number wasn't responding.

# *Family and Friends through the years*

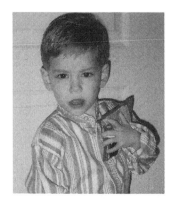

# 22

## Lightning does strike twice

My life carried on as it should for the next few years and in 2018 I received the devastating news that the last of my brothers, Monty, had passed away not long after a major stomach operation. Monty was nearly ten years younger than myself. Of the nine sons in our family of thirteen I was the surviving male.

In November 2018 I paid my G.P. a visit after finding that I was having trouble swallowing food. After checking on my symptoms and asking a few questions the doctor in question made an urgent referral to the main local hospital. After undergoing certain rigorous tests and body scans I was found to have a tumour in my oesophagus that was tested positive. As I had already suffered throat cancer in 1994 and been treated with radiotherapy for six weeks solid, attending clinic for the following twenty years and then being told they didn't want to see me again, everything was clear, I was totally dumbfounded not to say devastated.

My family and I have met with several specialists in discussing the course of treatment and because of the damage done by the radiotherapy in 1994/5 I have been advised that chemotherapy can help by hopefully being able to shrink the tumour. I don't know what the outcome will be of any treatment as apparently it has spread to the lymph nodes in my neck and I've been told that they cannot cure the cancer.

It's now Feb 2019 and I'm waiting for confirmation of when treatment will start and I guess everything is crossed at the moment. Halfway through March 2019 and I've had three cycles of chemotherapy. I attended hospital on 2nd of April for a scan and as to the results after the treatment, I'm pleased to say that it hasn't spread and has been contained. As a maximum of six cycles is advised I have decided to carry on with further chemo in the hope that results will improve or stabilise the condition. This will mean a period of no treatment to be decided by my doctor. This could be the start of remission if results are positive.

It's now the end of August 2019 and I have returned to the hospital for tests. As a result I have been told that I will need to have a further 9 chemotherapy sessions, starting in early September, in order to shrink the tumour. So, here I go again with a positive attitude I'm hoping that this treatment will be successful.

# 23

## Braunston – "Farewell Mr John"

As I am coming to the conclusion of my journey through my life my last venture was on 29th June 2019. I had a yearning to go back again in time to re-visit the village of Braunston. With the help of my daughter Dawn and son Kevin and their respective partners, I revisited the village to where I was evacuated for the duration of the war. Being there from the age of three and a half to the age of nine, it felt like my home.

I must admit that for me this was a very emotional and physically draining weekend. On getting together with those who I'd shared my young days, I didn't recognise anyone by their appearance or face but we all remembered what we did and got up to as youngsters.

On this visit I and my family were welcomed with open arms and one gentleman said, "Don't you remember me, we were best friends." Then, as on my last visit, the memories came flooding back and there were a few tears and some laughter too. I made a point of visiting the local church where as a kid I lived next door.

I wanted to find the resting place of the wonderful people who more or less adopted me on arrival in Braunston at the age of three and a half years. This I did and said a silent prayer over their graves, "Farewell, Mr John." All the family were laid to rest there together, John, Mary and daughter Isabel and last but not least dear Elizabeth, to me, Aunt Liz, with whom I spent the last year or so of the war.

Elizabeth's cottage has now been transformed and is unrecognisable as the home I lived in. I decided to do what I felt I needed to do. Knocking on the door I was welcomed by a young lady who after hearing my story invited me in and called her husband to join us. Wow, what a welcome, he literally dragged me in and wanted to hear my story as, to him, it was a piece of the history of the house. They had two lovely young children, a girl of seven and a boy of ten who also seemed very interested. He showed me around the house but I have to say, it wasn't the same for me, there were additions and an extension, however I did feel a kind of closeness and a feeling of a kind of spiritual presence, which brought a shudder to me. After forty minutes or so I felt ready to leave the house and thanked the occupants for their warm hospitality. The people I visited also ran a bed and breakfast property so we stayed overnight in two different buildings.

On the Sunday morning after breakfast we planned to spend some time touring around the village and visited the Plough pub for a quick refreshment stop before our journey home. The drivers refrained from alcohol, much to their chagrin.

The journey home took just one and a half hours and it's always nice arriving back home. I guess planning ahead now is not something I can do as another course of treatment starts again in September. I feel this is as good a time as any to bring my story to a close.

My story started at the age of three and I now bring it to a close at aged eighty-three.

A letter written by me to the people of the village of Braunston where I spent my very young days and the duration of the war

## BRAUNSTON 80 YEARS AGO - Memories of being evacuated at the start of the Second World War

As a 3 year old I didn't understand why I was being taken from my home to go and live in the countryside. It was 1939 and was to be an adventure that I shall never forget. I was taken to the picturesque village of Braunston in the smallest and prettiest county in England, Rutland.

I found myself in the local Manor House along with other children of my age. There were older couples there sizing us up and asking questions. A gentleman and a lady asked me if I would like to go and live with them. They seemed a very nice and kind couple and I said yes. I was one of the last to be chosen. They took my hand and said "Come along home, we're going home now. There was a small car outside which I learned later was an Austin Ruby. The car belonged to the gentleman I was going to live with: he was John Addison and the lady was his sister Mary. We drove just down the road to a farm where I was to spend the next four years of my life. I was also introduced to a very pretty young lady, who also lived there, called Isobel.

During my life on the farm I was enrolled in the local school where I met the friends I am visiting today. 29th June 2015. They became part of my life and we created a friendship and a bond that will always be with me. I was obviously a war time evacuee in all I spent five years in Braunston until the end of the war, when I was once again torn from the family who looked after me.

Incidentally all three people who I lived with have passed on but never forgotten. I want to thank you all for welcoming me to your community and I will treasure your friendship for the rest of my life. To John and Cassie and all the friends that are here today and those who have passed on. Thank you all from the bottom of my heart. You are indeed my family.

Ronald E. Heighs

# The Bedford Family (my mum's family)

George Bedford 1914 - 1918

JACK BEDFORD
19·14 - 1918

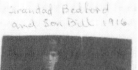

Grandad Bedford
and Son Bill 1916

George 1914
Bedford - 1918